THE
ENGLISH
SPIRIT

WINSTON CHURCHILL

[*Frontispiece.*

THE
ENGLISH SPIRIT

J. B. Priestley—Sir Philip Gibbs
Philip Guedalla—Somerset Maugham
Sir Hugh Walpole
and others

edited with an introduction by
ANTHONY WEYMOUTH

" *We must be free or die, who speak the tongue*
That Shakespeare spake ; the faith and morals hold
Which Milton held."—WILLIAM WORDSWORTH

Essay Index Reprint Series

BOOKS FOR LIBRARIES PRESS
FREEPORT, NEW YORK

First Published 1942
Reprinted 1972

Library of Congress Cataloging in Publication Data

Cobb, Ivo Geikie, 1887-   ed.
    The English spirit.

    (Essay index reprint series)
    "Talks...broadcast in the Empire service of the
British Broadcasting Corporation."
    Reprint of the 1942 ed.
    1. National characteristics, English--Addresses,
essays, lectures. 2. England--Civilization--Addresses,
essays, lectures. I. Title.
[DA118.C6 1972]   914.2'03   70-167437
ISBN 0-8369-2677-3

PRINTED IN THE UNITED STATES OF AMERICA
BY
NEW WORLD BOOK MANUFACTURING CO., INC.
HALLANDALE, FLORIDA 33009

CONTENTS

5

ILLUSTRATIONS

Anthony Weymouth

INTRODUCTION

I

THESE TALKS WERE broadcast in the Empire Service of
the B.B.C. and, with a few exceptions, in a series called
" To Talk of Many Things." The idea was to give
listeners an occasional relaxation from News Bulletins, War
Commentaries, and the like. The subjects were chosen
from as wide a field as possible. No effort was made to
select topics which would illustrate the English Spirit, and
yet when I looked through the Talks I was struck by the
light they threw on various aspects of the English character.
It occurred to me that to publish in book-form a selection
from this programme would make interesting reading and
give some idea of the Talks which were being broadcast
to listeners overseas. I think it is worth recording that
most of these Talks were given at a time when London was
in the throes of her greatest peril, when she was being
bombed and hourly expecting to be invaded. As, day
after day, I listened to the calm voices describing some
typically English scene—such, for instance, as the garden
with the fat yellow primroses which J. B. Priestley de-
scribes—I felt sure that Talks such as these must inspire
confidence in our Dominions and Colonies.

2

The Brains Trust was recently asked the question: how
should the written word differ from the spoken word?
Sir Patrick Hastings gave it as his view that there is only
one possible method of preparing a speech, and that is to

make no notes of any kind and not to write one word before you speak. Commander Campbell's answer was that the spoken is different from the written word because in the case of the first you have the help of intonation. Professor C. E. M. Joad said: " Campbell hit the nail on the head as usual. When you are writing you cannot rely on intonation to arouse emotion or to make the point . . . and therefore when you are writing, your words have to be very much more carefully chosen, your sentences very much more carefully balanced, since you have to rely for your effect purely upon the written word."

This, of course, is quite true. It is obvious that a speaker can influence the written word by the way he handles it and links it up with its associated words. But should there be a specialised technique for use when writing words which are subsequently to be spoken? And is a script written specially for reading aloud equally suitable for reading to oneself? If the answer to the second question is yes, then why should not all prose be as pleasing to read as to listen to? It therefore amounts to this. Do we need two distinct styles, one for the eye and the other for the ear? And, finally, is a special technique needed to produce a script suitable for the microphone?

3

In his essay " On familiar style " Hazlitt writes:

" Many people mistake a familiar for a vulgar style, and suppose that to write without affectation is to write at random. . . . To write a genuine familiar or truly English style, is to write as any one would speak in common conversation, who had a thorough command and choice of words, or who could discourse with ease, force, and perspicuity, setting aside all pedantic and oratorical flourishes. . . . You do not assume indeed the solemnity of the pulpit, or the tone of stage-declamation; neither are you at liberty to gabble on at a venture, without emphasis or discretion, or to resort to vulgar dialect or clownish pronunciation."

Now, it seems to me that here Hazlitt indicates the essence of clear writing. He regards a " truly English style " as one you would use in common conversation. Not for ordinary conversation are the rhetorical flourishes of the platform, the rounded periods of the sermon, or the orotundity of the bench or bar. And if what Hazlitt says of the written word was true in his day, how much more is it true for the word, the clause, the sentence which is intended for that most revealing instrument—the microphone?

The eighteenth and nineteenth century had a taste for the rococo, and this taste affected much of the prose writing. You have only to read, more or less at random, much of the writing of those days to realise that, to our minds, it is unnatural, pompous, and artificial. The turgid construction, the long sentences, the florid style may impress by their substance, but they oppress by their weight.

4

Now consider the following passage:

" She really seems to have been a very charming young woman, modest, generous, affectionate, intelligent and sprightly; a royalist, as was to be expected from her connections, without any of that political asperity which is as unwomanly as a long beard; religious, and occasionally gliding into a very pretty and endearing sort of preaching; yet not too good to partake of such diversions as London afforded under the melancholy rule of the Puritans, or to giggle a little at a ridiculous sermon from a divine who was thought to be one of the great lights of the Assembly at Westminster; with a little turn of coquetry, which was yet perfectly compatible with warm and disinterested attachment, and a little turn for satire, which yet seldom passed the bounds of good nature."

This example of the written word is taken from Macaulay's Essay on Sir William Temple. It is, of course, a good example of the prose of that day. It would make a shocking broadcast. It offers to the reader a clear picture of Dorothy Osborne; but to the listener who cannot turn back to re-read what he has failed to understand, it is an impossible sentence. It takes about a minute to read aloud, and even the most experienced broadcaster would find it difficult to deliver this one sentence in such a way that his listeners were clear in their own minds as to whether, for instance, it was Dorothy and not the divine who had " a little turn of coquetry."

To illustrate my argument that this kind of sentence is unsuitable for broadcasting, let me suggest how Macaulay's sentence might with advantage be rewritten for the microphone.

" Dorothy Osborne seems to have been a very charming young woman. She was modest, generous, affectionate, intelligent, and sprightly. She was a royalist, as you might expect from her connections; but she had none of that bitterness which is as unsuitable for a woman as a long beard. Dorothy was religious. She occasionally slipped into a rather attractive sort of preaching. But yet she was not too good to take part in such pleasures as London afforded—they were few, because the city was at that time under the straight-laced rule of the Puritans. She could even giggle at a ridiculous sermon from a clergyman who was considered to be one of the great lights of the Assembly at Westminster. To conside another side of her character: Dorothy Osborne could flirt, and yet her flirtations didn't prevent her from forming more lasting friendships. She could be sarcastic when she liked, yet her satire was seldom ill-natured."

Now, this rearrangement of Macaulay's prose makes it more suitable for broadcasting. It gains immeasurably in ease of delivery. Each sentence contains one idea. The listener should not find himself puzzled as to the meaning of any clause or its relationship to what was said before or after. The purist may object to one colloquialism—" didn't " instead of " did not." But from the conversational standpoint the detached negative is an abomination. The rearrangement makes, I submit, just as good reading as the original version and is incomparably better material for the voice. And yet the alterations are trivial, and consist mainly in the substitution of several short sentences for one long one, though it is true that a word has been changed here and there ; " flirtation," for example, for " coquetry." The complete revision of punctuation would, no doubt, be of greater service to the new broadcaster than to the speaker who is experienced in microphone technique. For, whereas the liberal supply of full-stops would indicate gently but firmly to the uninitiated that he must break up his sentences and pause at frequent intervals, the man familiar with this art would do so in any case.

5

The audience you address in a Talk may well amount to many millions, yet you will be wise to say what you have to say as if you were speaking to a lone person sitting by his fireside. Hundreds of people sitting at close quarters in a hall, seeing swarms of their fellow creatures around them, know that there is, there can be, nothing intimate about the relationship between them and the speaker, whereas the relationship between listener and broadcaster is the exact opposite of this. The broadcaster is talking to an individual, and therefore his approach to him must be intimate. He cannot establish this without two essentials: the first is a script written in conversational language; the second is a style of speaking which is (or, at any rate, approximates to) the style he would use in everyday conversation.

As to the first, the man who can construct a script which is really suitable for broadcasting is the lineal descendant of the essay writer. Before the miracle of radio transmission burst upon the world, the essay held the field as one of the most intimate, if not the most intimate form of communication between a writer and the person he addressed. From the days of Montaigne, with his friendly, almost affectionate approach—" Reader, loe here is a well-meaning booke . . . it is myselfe I pourtray "—to the intimacies of Lamb, the essay has always been the means by which a man unburdened himself of his thoughts, his reflections, and sometimes his troubles.

Now, it has been said that an essayist cannot hide himself and his characteristics from his readers, as a writer of poetry, of fiction, or of history can. For the essayist gives away his personal tastes and predilections by the choice of his subjects. He shows the kind of man he is by his approach to them, by his handling of his material, by the way he condemns one attitude and praises another. He leaves the reader a clear picture of himself, a picture which, if the essay is to be a good one, cannot be wilfully faked. For sincerity is the essence of a good essay.

6

To move forward in time from Montaigne and Bacon to the twentieth century and its ubiquitous radio services, we find exactly the same requisite for a good Talk—it must sound sincere. And to *sound* sincere it must *be* sincere. It is said, and I believe with truth, that a speaker cannot conceal his real personality from the microphone. What he is, this delicate instrument exposes. Is he nervous? Tiny inflexions of voice, which would pass unnoticed in ordinary conversation, are picked up by the microphone and, while not actually magnified or distorted, are rendered unmistakable. Is he by nature conceited, over-sure of himself, irritable or impatient of criticism? Trust the microphone to give him away. A broadcaster cannot " put across " a false personality, for any attempt at dissimulation would break down as the speaker became absorbed in his task.

A psychologist, I suppose, would say that a convincing broadcaster *projects* his personality into the microphone. This, I think, is indeed the case, and is also the reason why any attempt to present an artificial personality is bound to fail. For projection is an unconscious process and one which cannot be influenced to any extent by conscious interference. This is not to say that the way a broad-caster delivers his material is not in his control—that would be a ridiculous assertion. What is meant is that, like cheerfulness, the real characteristics of the broadcaster's personality keep breaking in. In the forefront are the elementary and superficial tricks, whimsicalities and mannerisms; behind these is the pattern of the real man. Long practice and much thought can unquestionably make it possible for a speaker to develop a particular type of microphone personality. But in doing so he alters his SELF, using the word in the sense in which William James defines it. It is clear that a man can improve his skill at anything by practice, and broadcasting is no exception. The conversational style, which is essential to the success of a Talk, can be natural to a speaker or it can be acquired by long and arduous work. The natural broadcaster is the exception rather than the rule. The ordinary man placed in front of the microphone wishes to be and to sound natural, but finds that an audience, whether living or symbolised by the microphone, tends to make this difficult. Unconsciously he braces himself, he squares his shoulders and clears his throat. These are bad pre-

liminaries to the successful performance of a task to which
a natural, easy state of mind is essential.

7

And this brings me to what I consider one of the main
essentials to the delivery of a good script, namely that the
speaker must himself experience the emotion and flavour
of the lines he is speaking. If he is describing an amusing
situation, he must sound amused; he must share the joke
with the listener. And he can do this most convincingly
if he himself is amused. Eleanora Duse admitted that
when she was acting an emotional part, she herself
experienced the emotions she was portraying. (I refrain
from entering into a discussion of the James-Lange
theory.)   A broadcaster, if he wishes to sound convincing,
will be well advised to picture a single listener with whom
he is having a conversation.   I repeat that his matter must
be simple, for the other partner in the process is unable to
stop him and ask for any particular point to be explained
or amplified. His words must be carefully chosen;
whenever possible a word of one syllable is preferable to
one of two or more. An appropriate word has often to
be sacrificed to one that is perhaps less apt but also less
liable to distortion. The other day, for instance, a script
I read contained the word " imperturbable." It was just
the right word, so far as the meaning went, but the clang
between the second and third syllables made it unsuitable
for speaking. I suggested substituting the word " calm."
Each sentence must be as simple as it is possible to make it.
Short, crisp sentences are the best. Subordinate clauses
should be strictly rationed. Paragraphs matter little, if
at all. The speaker who is absorbed in what he is saying
will need no paragraph. In point of fact, its sole use in a
broadcast script is to make the script easier for others to
read. The writer of a broadcast Talk should beware of
the extravagant use of adjectival or adverbial phrases.

As they never contain a finite verb, they are dependent for
their meaning on the clause to which they are attached.
They are apt, therefore, to hold up the sentence, even to
confuse the listener if they are sprinkled freely among the
text.   Some practised broadcasters produce a script which
is marked with hieroglyphics signifying short pauses,
times at which to breathe, and longer breaks.   Howard
Marshall, a most practised and popular microphone
figure, writes scripts which are little more than a series
of short statements.   But punctuation matters little in
his case: what is written down is merely a guide, and
this original method of punctuation has one advantage
—it tends to encourage a conversational delivery and to
discourage a tendency to read the script.

Careful punctuation may even be a liability to the
broadcaster, if he pays *too* meticulous an attention to
his full-stops.   Punctuation should, to a large extent, be
treated somewhat cavalierly by the speaker at the microphone.   Some experts, indeed, purposely disregard their
full-stops.   They pause, not at the end of the period, but
at some convenient comma in the succeeding sentence.
They join one sentence into another, their contention
being that as this invariably happens in ordinary conversation, it will lend verisimilitude to a broadcast.   I
must admit that the use of this device has a good deal
to recommend it, but, like other tricks, it should not be
used over much.

8

If the style is the man, we certainly need a distinctive
style for the man at the microphone.   Although in some
respects there is a tendency for the speech of today to be
the written word of tomorrow, there will, I daresay, always be found a use for a style of writing which, while
pleasant to read, is too intricate for conversation.   The
man who acquired his style in the days before broadcast-

ing should remember Somerset Maugham's comment on his own search for a literary style. "I took care how I placed my words," he writes, "but did not reflect that an order that was natural at the beginning of the eighteenth century was most unnatural at the beginning of ours."

I am inclined to think Mr. Bernard Shaw has succinctly summed up style when he says: "Effectiveness of assertion is the alpha and omega of style." This seems to me to be equally true for a broadcast.

There is, perhaps, one other point which is worth mentioning. The broadcaster would do well to retain in his script those figures of speech which have inadvertently slipped in—either because he dictated his Talk or because he was writing as he would speak—but which shock him when his eye falls on them in all the clearness of the written word. The modern use of the word "awful," both in its adjectival and adverbial form, is one instance. If you were describing, for instance, an evening spent at a friend's house, you would probably use some such expression as "We had an awfully jolly party." Now, if your eye falls on this phrase your first tendency would be to substitute some wording of which the purist would approve, such as "I spent a pleasant evening." But if you succumb and alter your script, you will scarcely avoid sounding stilted. And while your listener is accustomed to *read* your second version, he is equally accustomed to *hear* the version you originally wrote. And it is undoubtedly true that you can best hold his attention by talking to him in the language he is accustomed to hear.

Time has, of course, given an entirely different meaning to a word like "awful." I am reminded of a story my mother used to tell me. My grandfather, who lived in the days when both writing and conversation were more correct, if less free and easy, once heard my mother as a young woman refer to some event or person as "awfully jolly." The old gentleman beckoned her to the side of the easy chair in which he was sitting. " My dear child," he said gently, " nothing is awful but the Judgment Day."

While I adhere to my dictum that a combination of a good script and the right delivery is necessary for the perfect broadcast Talk, I am prepared to admit that a deficiency in the one can, to some extent, be remedied by perfection in the other. A serious subject can carry more of the academic and less of the conversational style than, for instance, a " News from Home," which is more or less the radio equivalent of a gossip column. I hold that when a bishop or a field-marshal broadcasts, we may reasonably expect him to sound like a bishop or a field-marshal. But there is no reason why he should not be easy to follow and friendly in his approach to his subject. In a word, he can unbend without losing his dignity or interfering with the picture of the speaker which the listener has formed in his mind.

9

It should perhaps be added that the Talks in this volume were all transmitted by short-wave across the oceans. Reception is variable, sometimes as good as on the medium wave or long wave; at other times it ranges from poor to bad. To meet, so far as possible, the uncertainty of reception and to enable listeners to hear short-wave programmes, even if the conditions at the time are unfavourable, broadcasters in the Empire Service are asked to speak slowly and distinctly; they are warned not to lower the power of their voice at the end of a sentence, as is usual in ordinary conversation. Those with special experience of short-wave reception report that programmes are sometimes heard through a screen of noise due, of course, to static interference; but they agree that it is usually possible for anyone speaking distinctly to be audible even when interference is severe.

It is perhaps fair to admit that no final opinion as to

B

the best methods of speaking over short-wave has yet been agreed upon.　But even in the last year short-wave reception has vastly improved, owing in part to more powerful transmitters, in part to improved receivers, and in part to careful rehearsal and production of the individual speaker.

This, and the fact that since 1939 we in Britain have been the centre of interest to the Dominions and the United States, have led to an ever-increasing number of listeners to the B.B.C. short-wave programmes.　It would be no exaggeration to say that thanks to the miracle of radio the outlying parts of the British Commonwealth have kept in almost as close touch as if they were in the continent of Europe instead of being separated by thousands of miles of sea.

One last reflection.　These Talks will serve, I hope, to prove to those who come after us that the English Spirit was very much alive in British Broadcasting during England's greatest hour of danger.

Philip Guedalla

MR. CHURCHILL

WE ARE NOT good at anniversaries in England. When I
come to think of it, almost the only one large numbers of
us manage to remember without a conscious effort refers
to an over-zealous gentleman named Guy Fawkes, who
carried the national weakness for grumbling at the
Government a little too far by placing large quantities of
gunpowder under the House of Commons. He may have
meant well. But he always strikes me as a bit of a Fifth
Columnist; and, anyway, the occasion seems hardly
worthy to supply us with our leading, if not our only,
anniversary.

I always feel our deficiencies in this respect, when I
start to wander about any Latin town in Europe or
America and find that half the streets and all the squares
are named after the Third of January or the Fourteenth of
October or some other glorious date in the nation's
history. The only date that any Englishman ever
remembers is quarter-day, when he has to pay his rent.
But when I fail to cash a cheque somewhere in the United
States, because it happens to be Lincoln's Birthday or
George Washington's and all business has been stopped in
honour of the occasion, I begin to wonder if that is really
the best way to glorify our great men. I mean, nobody
did nearly so much about it while they were alive. Both
of them had to fight every inch of the way against the
opposition of some of their own supporters in order to make
their historic contribution to the nation's growth; and, on
the whole, it seems to me that the right time to honour a
man's birthday is when you hope, in all sincerity and for

the public interest, that he may be going to have a great many more of them.

That is the way with an anniversary that falls on Sunday, November 30th, Mr. Winston Churchill's birthday. I suppose no man laid, or will ever lay, his country under a deeper obligation than the man who took office as Prime Minister on the very day the Germans broke into Western Europe and who helped to steady the British peoples through the anxious summer weeks of 1940, when they stood utterly alone. If they had gone down, a great deal more than England would have gone down with them. Freedom and decency, life, liberty, and the pursuit of happiness throughout the world hung in the balance, as the slight barrier of Britain stood in the path of a barbarian invasion which had swept Western Europe in a month. Things are very different today, with Britain armed again and the three greatest human units in the world—the British Empire, the United States, and the Soviet Union—linked in a common purpose to put Germany back where it belongs. But I wonder if things would have been so different without one man to say what Englishmen were thinking and to do what Britain wanted done in the hot summer weeks of 1940. I doubt it. That is why the anniversary I mentioned is of interest to a good many million people outside Great Britain and the British Empire. It is a good thing for all free men, wherever they may live, that Mr. Churchill has a birthday, and we wish him many more.

All public men are remembered as they were at one particular moment of their lives. They may have spent long years in getting to that moment and long years after it. But history will always think of Wellington as a level-headed man of forty-six on a wet Sunday morning in June, 1815, and on horseback, and on the ridge of Waterloo; and of Lincoln in the instant of straightening himself up to deliver the Gettysburg Address; and of Gladstone as a fierce old man—half Major Prophet and half force of nature—pleading the cause of Ireland when he was over eighty. He was not always eighty. He had been in public life for nearly sixty years and pleaded a great many other causes. But that is how he is remembered, as we shall always remember Mr. Churchill for the sound of his voice speaking to his countrymen in that summer of 1940, when Great Britain stood in greater peril than at any moment in its history, knew it, and (thanks, perhaps, to Mr. Churchill) rather liked it.

His training to perform that supreme service had been a long business. He started as a cavalry subaltern. So, incidentally, did Chatham: it seems to be a good beginning. As there was not enough for subalterns to do, he turned himself into a war correspondent in order to see active service on the North-West Frontier. Then he made what he saw there into a book; and its success showed him that there might be a good deal more for him to do in life than drill Hussars and play regimental polo. But life in the 4th Hussars had given him a sight of India. After that he went with the 21st Lancers to the Sudan and tasted the doubtful pleasure of riding in a cavalry charge. There are not many men in public life who have ridden in a charge of cavalry. We used to hear a lot from Mussolini and Hitler about their military careers. Mr. Churchill does not seem to talk about his quite so much; but, then, Mr. Churchill really was a soldier. After the Sudan he went on to South Africa and touched another corner of the military career by finding out what it is like to be a prisoner of war. He was not one for very long, because he preferred to escape. But he brought away with him a lifelong sympathy with imprisoned persons, which he applied to some purpose as a prison reformer when he was Home Secretary.

People sometimes say that politicians will do anything for votes. But there are not many votes in prison reform.

You lose the warders', and the convicts have not got any; and when Mr. Churchill found his feet in politics, he was less influenced in favour of what might be popular than of what he thought was right. It was not particularly popular to fight hard for naval appropriations before the last war, to scrape for expenditure on the first development of the Naval Air Service, to get something going in the teeth of departmental sceptics which actually grew into the first tank that we ever had. But Mr. Churchill did all those things because he happened to believe in them—and he was right.

It was not particularly popular to warn the sleeping world of the democracies before the present war of the uncomfortable fact that there might be trouble coming. There are shorter cuts to popularity than the enunciation of unpleasant truths; and nobody loves the bringer of bad news. But Mr. Churchill has never looked for short-cuts to popularity. Indeed, the chief thing about him has always been a dangerous aptitude for saying what he thought, regardless of the consequences. (He got that from his father; but his mother was an American, so he may have got it from her too.)   That healthy practice is probably the reason why he has spent a fair proportion of his public life as a lone wolf in politics. He is the chosen leader of a great party now. But he has often had to play a lone hand outside the obedient ranks of any party; and as the glory of democracy is the Independent rather than the good party man, he looks like the right man to defend it.

And he seems to be the man to do it. He was trained to war. The greater part of his official life was spent in the study of war problems—at the Admiralty before and during the last war and for the first eight months of this one; at the Ministry of Munitions in 1917 and 1918, when our production reached the volume which bore the Germans down; and at the War Office for two years after the war. Nearly all his writings deal with military subjects. Admiral Lord Fisher, even when he disagreed with him, called Mr. Churchill a " War Man " and testified that his " audacity, courage, and imagination specially fitted him to be a War Minister." We knew all that about him. But what came as rather a surprise to some people was his ability to transmit his courage to others. No 'one ever doubted his. There was the apocryphal story of the cautious general who came to Colonel Churchill's headquarters in France, when he was commanding a battalion in the line in 1916 and pointed out that it was in " a very dangerous place." " Yes, sir," said Colonel Churchill, " but, after all, this is a very dangerous war."

He used to fly across to France when he was Minister of Munitions, and once the engine failed over the Channel. He began to wonder how long they would be able to keep afloat and felt what he described to someone as " a curious calm." They asked him afterwards if he had been afraid of dying. " No," he said. " I love life, but I don't fear death." That is a leader for a nation at war.

He has the nerve; he has the knowledge; he knows what it is all about; he has seen the world of which the future hangs in the balance. America, Africa, and Asia have all seen something of Mr. Churchill in their time. When he was at the Admiralty, he cruised incessantly to see things for himself. He always likes to see things for himself; and that is just as well, because the curse of modern times is the untravelled politician. Just how much of the world has Hitler ever seen ? Precisely nothing, outside his country, a muddy trench or two in France in the last war, some streets in Italy lined with Mussolini's plain-clothes men, and the back areas of German armies. That is not a foundation on which you can rebuild the world; and half his contemporaries are not much better. Next time a man begins to tell you how he would reorganise the world after the war, ask him if he has ever been there.   Mr. Churchill has.

One sometimes forgets his immense official experience. He has been Home Secretary; he has been Chancellor of the Exchequer; he has been President of the Board of Trade; he has been Secretary for the Colonies and Dominions.   But, above all, he has moved freely up and down the world for the best part of two generations. When he was a child, he knew that the United States were not a large pink surface on a map, but the place his mother came from.   He was in New York on his way to see the war in Cuba before he was twenty-one; he was lecturing there with Mark Twain as his introducer before he was thirty.   He learned something of the East in India and Egypt.   The war in South Africa taught him to respect the South African Burghers. The first free constitutions of the Transvaal and Orange River Colonies were introduced in the House of Commons by a young Under-Secretary named Churchill; and when Louis Botha came to London, the General reminded him that they had " been out in all weathers."   One rainy afternoon, indeed, they had not been very far from shooting one another in Natal.

Experience of peace and war, experience of men and nations—that has been Mr. Churchill's training for leadership.   But his main quality is something nobody can teach; the quality that made a Spaniard not so long ago, when speaking of him and remembering the bull-ring, say " *Qué toro* "—" What a bull for a fight."   Half English, half American, and wholly trained to war, he has a birthday, and we wish him many more.

PHILIP GUEDALLA

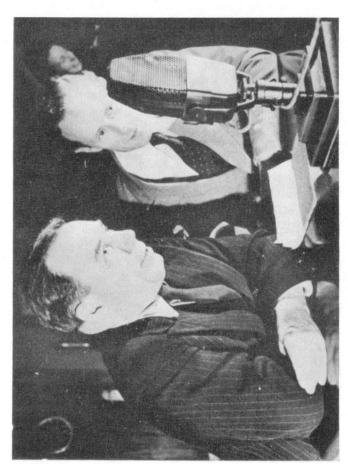

J. B. PRIESTLEY AND LESLIE HOWARD

J. B. Priestley

THIS LAND OF OURS

I DON'T KNOW whether it's the long, hard winter we've had, one of the worst in living memory, or whether it's the effect of the war, but I never remember England looking lovelier than it's done this month. I've stared at it as if I'd never seen a spring. I have a house down in the Isle of Wight, which is a sort of miniature Southern England, and what I've seen round that house lately has taken my breath away. To begin with, it's all *greener* than ever this year. Everywhere an incredible variety, lushness and tenderness of green. And we've had all the blossom out —apple, cherry and peach—perfectly set against the weather-stained old walls; a blaze of tulips; and along the little stream by the tennis court the fattest and yellowest primroses I ever remember seeing. Then behind the twinkling new leaves of the old elms you could see the misty green curves and slopes of the Downs, almost melting into the blue. Then swallows and martins flashing about; blackbirds singing exquisitely from morning till night; and cuckoos calling around the house—and I'll swear there have never been so many before—those wandering voices that turn the world again into a fairy place. There's been a kind of magical spell over our country, as if we saw it at last, now that we must give up everything to defend its liberty, its traditions, its very life, in its full enchantment.

One of the most absurd things Shakespeare ever did was to pretend that his " Midsummer Night's Dream " was set in Athens and its neighbourhood. Actually nothing was ever more English than this " Midsummer

25

Night's Dream." It's a kind of lovely mad picture of the English scene, of the English tradition, of the English mind and spirit. The whole odd mixture of the thing is so English. What do you get in it? Well, in the foreground a lot of rather cosy domestic stuff, lovers quarrelling and comic characters like Bottom and Weaver and Quince and Snug and Starveling all enjoying themselves, all homely and comfortable, nothing grandiose. Now, all that in the foreground is very English, and may be said to represent one half of the English tradition, mind and spirit—cosy and comic and domestic—the England of the novelists, of the music-halls, of the cricket and football crowds. But the background of the "Midsummer Night's Dream" is different—the broken moonlight in the enchanted wood; the voices of fairy people; a vague loveliness, mystery, magic—occasionally suggested by lines that make your hair stand on end, they have such evocative beauty; lines like:

"Following darkness like a dream. . . ."

And this, to my mind, is the other half of England, of the English tradition and spirit. It is the England of the lyric poets and of the old water-colour painters and of such odd mystical figures as William Blake. All this is just as much part of us as the cosy domestic comedy in the foreground. "The Englishman," said the Spanish philosopher Santayana, "is governed by the weather in his soul." We are, you see, an instinctive and intuitive people. We don't act from clear-cut first principles. We haven't worked out a logic of living. We distrust the dialecticians. As a nation we often behave irrationally and so bewilder our friends just as we baffle our enemies, and our friends begin to imagine that we are a nation of grown babies, just as our enemies come to the conclusion that we are a set of cunning cold-blooded hypocrites. The truth is that both are wrong. What happens is that we fall under the spell

of that strange hazy background, the broken moonlight
in the enchanted wood, and we try obscurely to relate
everything to something deep inside us, something that is
half-moral, half-mystical, hoping that at last a decision
and a plan will grow naturally out of this deep soil, not
popping up like a telegraph-pole, but growing naturally
and strongly, adapting itself to all weathers, like a tree.

The strength of English life, political, social and intellectual, is that it has been allowed to grow like a tree.
Compared with a telegraph-pole—and the Totalitarian
States are like telegraph-poles—of course, it all looks
queer, twisted, ramshackled, and probably ready to come
down at any moment. But the tree is that shape because
it has adapted itself with infinite, patient adjustment to
meet every possible stress of wind and weather, and it is
alive and fruitful and after centuries of growth can still
put out fresh green leaves. This is what the German
mind, which is almost the exact opposite of the English
mind, can never understand. The German cannot
comprehend an instinctive political wisdom, a natural
sagacity on the part of men who have both to govern and
be governed. There is more sense of political life, of
reasonable government, in any English parish council
than there is in the whole German Reich. Though their
achievements in other directions are great enough, in this
world of government the Germans are a set of mad
babies. I will quote here some valuable words written
recently by a great German, Thomas Mann. He says:

" The German people cannot, in the last resort, blink
their eyes to the fact that England's attitude to power is
quite other, and incomparably more natural and straight-
forward, than the German attitude. Both parties understand something quite different by it—it is the same word
with a wholly different meaning. To Englishmen power
is in no way the darkly emotional concept as viewed by
Germans: power, in English eyes, implies no emotion—

the will to power is a German invention—but a function: they exercise it in the gentlest and most unobtrusive manner, with the least possible display, and safeguarding as much freedom as is feasible, for they do not believe that power is a proclamation of slavery, and are therefore not slaves to power themselves. This is called Liberalism—an old-fashioned word for a very vital thing. . . ."

This Liberalism, as Thomas Mann rightly calls it, is probably England's greatest contribution to world civilisation. It has been produced by an odd mixture of peoples living their own kind of life on a misty island just off the edge of the great European peninsula, a people who have been allowed by circumstances—and also by their own passion for liberty—to develop in their own way, to grow as a tree grows. It runs through all our political and social life, and not only here in this island but everywhere the English have gone. It runs through our glorious literature, in which there is blended an appreciation of the twists and turns of human character with a sense of the strange mystical background of this life, a blue haze like that we find so often over the English hills. It is there in our everyday life, in which everything on the surface is so illogical and absurd, so that we are for ever laughing at ourselves, but within there is sanity, there is deep kindness, there is a natural goodness. (Here we are in sharp contrast with the German, who is all shrewd sense and logic and efficiency on the surface, and bewildered and half-mad inside.) I'm not pretending we're faultless, or that everything is perfect here. I doubt if anybody has criticised this country and some of its people more frequently than I have during these past seven years, ever since the publication of my *English Journey*. But if I've shouted for things that I thought wrong to be put right, it's because I know how well worth the trouble this country and its people and traditions are, how nobly they can repay our passionate

care. Here is no rotten old tree, waiting for a pull or
two of a rope to come crashing down. Here is a grand
old oak, deeply and thickly rooted in its soil, twisted and
gnarled if you like, but still giving shade below and still
catching the sunlight and moonlight in its upper branches.
If this tree were uprooted, if it vanished from the wood
of the world, there would be such a terrible emptiness
there, such a desolation where there had once been such
sweetness and strength, that the world could never be the
same again and would have a tale to break men's hearts.
But it will not be uprooted. And what matters in the
end—and if it does not then the world is simply a hell
and the sooner we are all out of it the better—is downright goodness, the simple goodwill. Now I believe
this deep natural goodwill to be a notable characteristic
of our people. I remember last year a clever foreigner,
who knows us well, saying to me: "You know, the
English are a *good* people. When you come to know
them, you see there is something naturally, instinctively
religious about them." By *religious* he did not mean that
the English people are fonder of prayer, worship and ritual
than other people, for clearly they are not. He meant
that the ordinary English folk have an instinctive trust in
the moral order of the universe, have a deep respect for
all that is fundamentally personal to other people, and are
moved by goodwill. This goodwill runs like a golden
thread, glinting with humour and poetry, through the
fabric of our history. And I believe with all my heart that
it will be a black tragic day for the world when that
shining thread is seen no more; but I also believe that it
will outlast our time.

Sir Hugh Walpole

LOVE OF THE ARTS AND OF ENGLAND

I KNOW VERY well that the words " The Arts " have for
many people a priggish and suspicious sound.   I would
like in this talk to give a very simple explanation why, in
England at this particular moment, literature and painting and music are proving such stand-bys for myself and
many other people.

I have a little house in the Lake District with an acre of
ground, and I love this more than any other spot on
God's earth.   It is half-way up a little mountain, has a
lake at its feet, has a lawn on which the fattest and tamest
of thrushes strut like archbishops, has a rose garden, a
rock garden, bees, and a library with fifteen thousand
books.   All in one acre.

I mention this in no spirit of pride but for the following
reason.

One lovely June evening (and I am only one of many
that assert there has never been in England before a June
to surpass this one) I was sitting in the little book-lined
parlour looking out on to the garden when I listened to
the News—and the News that evening was terrible!

As I listened I realised that phenomenon common to us
all, when the stomach turns right over, the heart begins
to hammer at twice its proper pace, and the throat is dry
as with carraway seed.   What I needed, of course, was a
little time to see things in proper proportion, for this war
is a vast business that neither one defeat nor one victory
can possibly determine.   Ultimately I did see things in
proportion, and I may say that I have never known a

moment of panic since, but, on that beautiful evening when the air was still and there was no sound save the running of the stream through my garden and the sleepy friendliness of the bird-calls, for two hours or more I knew panic. My panic that evening, I am afraid, was selfish. I looked out on my acre of ground, and knew that it was all in this world, besides work, friends and health, that I wanted. I hope, when this war is over that there will be a new England and that every man will have his acre, but in any case, at that exact moment, I saw my acre taken from me, the Concentration Camp, the loss of my freedom.

Now, it happened that in my panic I had let the wireless run on and it had continued from the News into a Beethoven Trio. For a lot of people the names of Beethoven, Bach and Brahms have a stuffy highbrow sort of connotation. They oughtn't to have. For instance, on this particular evening this Trio contained the merriest, simplest little tune possible to the musical mind of man. Nothing could be simpler. I went the other evening to a performance of *Chu Chin Chow*, the musical fairy-tale that ran for four years at His Majesty's Theatre in London during the last war. I was present, as a matter of fact, at the very first night of it there ever was. I had not seen it since that first night, but the music now, although so inevitably familiar, was as fresh and charming as ever. The Beethoven Trio tune and " The Cobbler's Song " in *Chu Chin Chow* belong to the same family. Norton, for all I know, took his Cobbler's Song from Beethoven. Anyway, the Beethoven tune was as simple as that, and lovely and reassuring.

As I sat there listening, but miserable and frightened, I looked at a picture above my mantelpiece, a picture by the French painter Utrillo. It is my favourite among all the pictures in my possession. It represents a white wall and some houses in the street of a Southern French town.

There is great heat there and great coolness, too, but above all there is great peace. The white wall is wonderfully painted. I don't know how many shades of white are there, but all the beauty lies in its colour, its reality and its symbolism—the way that it stands, as poetry does, for all the beauty of nature and man's genius, however terrible the moment's events may be. It seemed to say: " Wait. Be patient. I am permanent." A voice in your ear saying: " Be still and know that I am God." Well, when the Beethoven was finished I got down from the shelf one of my favourite books. Dickens's *David Copperfield*. At least it *was* one of my favourites, but some six years ago I was in Hollywood and helped to write a script from the book for the films. That, I thought, had destroyed *David Copperfield* for me for ever. I felt that, not only did I know it by heart, but that I had wrangled so often and so crossly with others about Betsy Trotwood and Mr. Micawber and Uriah Heap that those characters were lost to me as human beings.

I opened it at random and began to read that immortal passage when David walks all the way to Dover to find his aunt. How well I remembered the filming of those scenes and how poor little Freddie Bartholomew, who was then little more than a baby, was made to do the scene when he stands outside the gate of his aunt's cottage and looks into the garden, over and over again, and how bravely he stood up to it.

However, although I knew the words so well that I could almost repeat them before I got to them, I was caught entirely away and read on until I came to that immortal and joyous scene when the Murdstones arrive to claim David, and Betsy Trotwood defies them, and Mr. Dick cries triumphantly: " Have him measured for a suit of clothes! " I had forgotten Hollywood, I had forgotten the war. My spirit was at peace.

I was restored to my right and tranquil mind that evening by a German musician of genius, a French painter of genius, an English writer of genius. I can't define genius, but I know that for one thing it extends beyond all boundaries of nations, all events of history, all prejudices and personal discontents.

I love my country with passion, and I think that every man and woman should love his or her country. I admit that when I look, as we all must do, to the world problems that will follow this war, I know that two opposites must be reconciled—my love of England and the necessity for some kind of world federation and companionship. I must give up *narrow* patriotism, but at the same time I want this acre of ground in Cumberland to be mine to plant flowers in and keep my trees strong and healthy, and tend my bees.

No easy problem. But the great artists of the world solve some of the problems for me. When I listen to the Fifth Symphony of Beethoven, it doesn't matter to me whether he was born a German or a Hottentot. Hamlet is every man in every part of the world. In the Renaissance the people of Florence honoured a picture by the painter Cimabue by making a great procession and carrying it through the streets, waving banners, scattering flowers, blowing trumpets. They were proud of course that Cimabue belonged to their country, but they were also proclaiming that the Arts were the freest, the most joyous, the friendliest of all the manifestations of man. Very different this from the burning of the books in Germany!

Like every other man, I have known great disappointments—in myself, my ambitions, my friends, world events—from time to time. But books have never disappointed me, pictures have radiantly encouraged me, music has carried me forward, fortifying and strengthening me.

The point, though, about these things just now is their

C

immortality. Nothing, no evil success, no momentary turn and twist of history, can destroy them. It is true, of course, that a bomb may wipe out my Utrillo, and my library of fifteen thousand books go up in one single flame. But the great paintings of the world are many, and if every volume of Shakespeare disappeared tomorrow he would be somewhere reconstructed, for he is built deep into the heart and soul of man. It goes, though, much deeper than that, for no Totalitarian ideology can crush the artistic fire of man. Man must always be creating beauty, and if it is not in one fashion it will be in another.

After I had put *David Copperfield* back on his shelf I went out into my garden, and the stars blazed in the sky above the lawn and the line of the very quiet little hills was dark and permanent against the cool night blue.

So those hills will remain, and the little tune from the Beethoven Trio, and David Copperfield looking over the gate into Betsy Trotwood's garden.

These are the things in which we may always trust.

H. E. Bates

THE ENGLISH COUNTRYSIDE

ONE MORNING, NOT long ago, I got up rather early and went out for a walk. It was a warm, sunny, very still morning—wonderfully still. No wind, just a few very high white clouds, like white brush-marks on the blue sky. In the night there had been a very heavy dew— one of those sopping, drenching dews that you so often get in the middle of summer in England. It lay thick on everything. It covered the trees and the hedgerows and the honeysuckle and the spiders' webs and the corn in the fields like millions of glass beads. Where the grass had been cropped short and fine by sheep, it looked like the bloom on a grape. And just now and then the sun-light would catch one of these glass beads of dew and it would flash just like a tiny electric lamp.

Apart from this and the occasional shaking of a bough as the dew fell off it, there was hardly any movement or sound at all as I walked down the narrow road from my house towards the woods half a mile away. The whole countryside was dead still with that deep tranquil summer silence that you can almost hear.

And then suddenly I saw something and I heard something. I saw what I thought was a white kitten running across the road. A white kitten with a fluffy tail. But it wasn't a white kitten. It was a white squirrel. Pure white, with tiny bright pink eyes. He almost bounded across the road, and then over a holly-bush and finally up into the branches of an oak-tree. I only got one more glimpse of him—flying high up among the wet leaves of the oak-tree—and then he was gone.

Pure white squirrels aren't, of course, very common in England, and I stood for some minutes longer, trying to get another look at this uncommonly beautiful little creature. And then I heard a sound. In contrast to the white squirrel it was one of the commonest, and I suppose oldest, sounds in the English countryside. It was the sound of someone sharpening a scythe.

I couldn't see this man who was sharpening his scythe, but I guessed what he was going to do. It was a little too late for hay-making, and I guessed that he must be going to mow a path for the binder in one of the first harvest-fields—oats most probably. The English harvest is early this year—and it's going to be good too, very good —and all over the land I could pick out fields of oats just turning ripe in the sun. A lot of oats have been grown in England this year, and they all look good. I haven't seen a bad field yet. And I think I like the look of oats almost more than any other English corn crop. I like the colour of them when they're ripe—not exactly yellow, not exactly white, not quite cream—but a sort of soft opal colour, with a touch of pink in the stem.

Actually, of course, there has been an increase, not only in the acreage of oats grown in England this year, but of almost every other crop. And we've got one or two new crops. Well, not really new. But new enough to the conservative English farmer. Flax is one of them. These fields of flax are a lovely sight. When the flowers are open in the sun the field looks from a distance like a piece of trembling blue water.

Yes, there are plenty of crops in England this year. Plenty of wheat and barley and oats. Plenty of roots. Plenty of potatoes—fields and fields of white and pink and purple potato-flowers with their orange centres shining above the dark foliage in the sun. In fact, if any of you were to come home and see the English country-side now, in time of war, that would be the change you'd notice most, I think. More growing crops, and less grass. That would be the thing that would strike you most— how the green fields have been ploughed up and sacrificed to the necessity of war. They say there's never any need for a revolution in England, because there's one going on all the time. And the ploughing up of the green fields is just a small part of that revolution.

But I want to get back for a moment to this early morning walk I was telling you about. I hadn't got up early just simply to look at the crops. What I'd really got up early for was to look for mushrooms. The English, as you know, are a very conservative people, and they eat only one sort of mushroom. There are at least fifty kinds they could eat, but they just won't, and they just don't, and that's all about it. The kind they eat has a pure silky white top and soft crushed-strawberry coloured gills underneath. It's got a delicious flavour, and when you see it growing in a green field, with the dew on it and the sun shining on the dew, it's very beautiful too.

And I think gathering mushrooms, in the later English summer, is one of the pleasantest, most tranquillising, most rejuvenating occupations in the world. Some of you who are listening, some of you who know England, must know only too well how pleasant it is ; how you wander in circles over the field, keeping your eye open for distant blobs of white, how you keep getting deceived by scraps of white thistledown, white paper, perhaps a white feather, a white flint, a white flower, until at last you see the firm, shining, unmistakable thing you're after. Some of you, perhaps, heard J. B. Priestley talking of how he found wonderful relaxation from the nervous strain of war by simply watching a few ducks swimming on a pond. I shall have something to say about ducks myself before this talk ends. But gathering mushrooms is rather like watching ducks. It takes you out of yourself. It has the same way of tranquillising and rejuvenating the mind.

Do you see what I'm trying to get at now, what I'm trying to show you? It's this—that morning, as I was gathering mushrooms, it occurred to me that that field and the landscape surrounding it, the oat-fields, the woods, the copses of sweet chestnut, the deep stretches of bracken under the birch-trees, the little lanes between the hedgerows of hawthorn and honeysuckle hadn't changed much for a hundred years. It was 1940; but it might just as easily have been 1840 or 1870, or 1900 or 1910.

But there was just one change. This field where I was walking was surrounded on all four sides by thick woods. At one end there was just a small opening between the trees. I suppose a very skilled pilot, at great risk, could have landed a 'plane in that field. But the farmer had taken no chances. I don't propose to tell you—and Mr. Hitler—precisely what defensive obstacles he had contrived, but my small son, when he saw them later, called them "knitting needles." And that's exactly what they look like—giant knitting needles —very uncomfortable things to stick into the underpart of any air invader who tries to land in the grass-fields and the corn-fields of this country.

And talking of invasion, I'd like to end this talk with a story of something that happened after I'd been for this early morning walk in the calm heavily dewed English countryside that war has so far changed so little.

After I'd gathered my mushrooms I walked back home. I said I had something to say about ducks. Well, I keep a few ducks—just a dozen to amuse my children and for the sake of a few eggs. But ducks have a way of laying away from home, and lately we hadn't been getting many eggs. So as I came home and passed the village pond where the ducks spend most of their time among the yellow water-lilies, I thought it might be a good idea to look there for some eggs.

Well, I searched round the pond without success. Finally there was only one place left—a small island towards the middle of it. So I decided to search that too. The water was too deep for wading and I had no boat. So I got out a ladder and made a bridge across from the bank to the island, and then crawled across it on my hands and knees.

You've heard a lot of talk, I dare say, about the invasion of England. Well, half-way across to this island in the pond, I discovered something of what it feels like to be the invader of an island. Because suddenly I discovered that that small island was defended.

It was defended by a wasps' nest. And as I perched there, on my very flimsy bridge, with four feet of muddy water underneath me, the advanced striking force of wasps bore on me with a series of very unpleasant attacks on the back of my neck.

There's no moral to this story. But I should just like to add this. I never got to that island, and I didn't get any eggs. And all the time I perched on that ladder, under fire so to speak, the ducks, for some reason or other, persisted in cackling loudly.

TWENTY DAYS IN A SHIP

ON MY RETURN from France a fortnight ago today, I gave a short talk on my journey home in a collier with five hundred refugees. Since then, among many other letters I have received a number from persons who said that they had no sympathy with us, and if we had suffered danger, discomfort and hardship during our escape, we thoroughly deserved it, for we had gone to the Riviera to lead idle, pleasure-loving lives, while our country was fighting for its existence. Well, sympathy is a commodity that does not cost much, but the persons who are short of it are very wise to hoard it till they have occasion to expend it on themselves. But I should tell you that I never saw a set of people who asked for sympathy less than the refugees who were crowded together for twenty days in that brave little collier. They were a cheerful crowd, notwithstanding all they had to put up with, and, what is more, a calm and courageous crowd.

But my correspondents who accused them of being idle pleasure seekers were, as it happens, completely wrong. Many of them were invalids who had lived on the Riviera for years for their health's sake. Many were retired military men and Indian civilians who, after spending a lifetime in the service of the State, had settled down in modest little houses in quiet corners of the coast. The State, as we know, does not pension its servants with an exaggerated generosity, and they could live there inexpensively. After many years in the tropics they could not stand the rigours of an English winter.

But the majority were people who had earned their

living there. There were gardeners, chauffeurs, governesses, teachers of English, clerks, tradesmen, hotel keepers, doctors and clergymen. Many of them had spent years building up some trade or business which provided them with a modest livelihood, and they were returning to England, ruined, with absolutely nothing to look forward to. You may wonder why these persons should have chosen to settle down away from their own country. Well, you know we British are not stay-at-home folk. For centuries we have wandered about the world, urged by our desire for the new and strange, and settled ourselves wherever we could find a foothold. We have always loved freedom and we have welcomed adventure. That is why great parts of the world's surface are now populated by English-speaking nations. That is why the Dominions and the Colonies are there to fight the good fight with us in defence of liberty, honour, truth and straight dealing.

We were a very democratic crowd; we all had to queue up together for our rations. We all had to sleep cheek to jowl in the holds or on the hatches. We all had to do our own sweeping and our own washing-up. We all had to share the same tub of soapy water to wash. A cargo of coal had just been discharged from the ship when she came to fetch us, and coal-dust was everywhere. Our hands and faces, our clothes, were grimy with it. Believe me, dirt very quickly makes all men equal; I don't see why cleanliness should not have the same effect, and I venture to express the hope that the new order, which we are all looking forward to after the war, will bring to all of us the possibility, among other things, of keeping clean. We shall truly be much more nearly equal if we can all make an equal use of soap and water.

I should like to tell you how we passed our days. They were long. We slept on iron decks with only a rug under us, and by six most of us were doing our best to wash. At half-past we got our tea ration. We had a

scanty breakfast at nine, a scanty dinner at one and a
scanty supper at six. We chatted to one another.
Queueing up for rations took a long time. We played
patience. Two or three of us would sit together with a
couple of grubby packs of cards, and onlookers, as they
always will, would give us unsolicited advice. Some of
us read. It interested me to see that most of us read
thrillers. It was curious, because of course we were
actually living a thriller. We never knew when we
settled ourselves down for the night whether we should
not be torpedoed before morning, and since we had no
rafts or lifebelts, and only boats sufficient for forty if
we were torpedoed, it was inevitable that the vast majority
of us would be drowned. Yet you saw people sitting
about the deck absorbed in adventures much more im-
probable and not nearly so exciting as our own. I had
had only an hour or so to get together the few things I
was able to take with me, and I had chosen two novels
because they were long and would take some time to
read. They were Thackeray's *Esmond* and Charlotte
Brontë's *Villette*. I had not read them for thirty years.
People will tell you that *Esmond* is dull. Well, I didn't
find it so. I thought it interesting, urbane and beautifully written. And in these times in which we are living
it is good to have it insisted upon that loyalty, honour,
courage and uprightness are the most valuable qualities
of man. I enjoyed *Villette* too. It is a trifle old-fashioned,
and the right person turns up in the right place with a
regularity that you find hard to believe. But the people
are living people and they are wonderfully interesting.
The third book I had I chose in a hurry, almost by chance.
It was the *Trial and Death of Socrates*. I had read it more
than once, but never had it seemed to me so moving as
when I read it in that ship, knowing that every day might
be my last. The noble words of Socrates had then a
peculiar meaning. " The difficulty, my friends," he

said, " is not to avoid death, but to avoid unrighteous-
ness; for that runs faster than death." And again,
" There is great reason to hope that death is good, for
one of two things—either death is a state of nothingness
and utter unconsciousness, or, as men say, there is a
change and migration of the soul from this world to
another. If death is like a sleep undisturbed even by
dreams," then, he says, " to die is gain, for eternity is
then only a single night. But if death is the journey to
another place, and there, as men say, all the dead abide,
what good, O my friends and judges, can be greater
than this."

I should like to tell you how this strange experience
affected the people who went through it. My impression
is that it exaggerated their natural characteristics. The
unselfish became more unselfish and kindly and eager to
help one another, and the selfish became more grossly
selfish. Of the latter I have a little story to tell which
may amuse you. Just before we arrived in Oran in
Algeria, a collection was made for the crew, and afterwards one lady went up to the steward and asked him to
give her a double ration that day. He said he was afraid
he couldn't. " But when the hat was passed round this
morning I put in a hundred francs," she said. " I really
think you might give me a double ration for that." The
steward was a Scot with a quick sense of humour. " I
really can't, Madam," he replied, taking a bank-note out
of his pocket, " but I shouldn't like to think you had
given the crew a gratuity, and for nothing in return, so
let me give you your hundred francs back."

There was a young man on board crippled by infantile
paralysis so that he couldn't get up and down the steep
ladder which was the only way into the hold in which
we slept. He had only been married a fortnight. Owing
to his disability he and his wife were given the hospital
to sleep in. This was a small cabin with three bunks.

Now, among the refugees there was an old woman of over eighty, the widow of the sexton at one of the English churches. She had lived in France for many years, and her only wish was to be allowed to die there, but her daughter was married to a Frenchman and they had persuaded her to go in the refugee ship. The shock, the heat, the anxiety were too much for the old woman, and her mind gave way. She spent her days babbling feebly and curling her thin white hair round her trembling fingers. Then it was plain that she was failing. She was put in the little hospital with the newly married couple. They slept in that cabin while she lay dying. They slept in that cabin when she lay dead. There was nowhere else for them to go. The sailors made a shroud for her from old sacking, and at midnight a clergyman hurriedly read the burial service by the light of a torch. The convoy stopped for one minute, not out of respect for the dead, there was no time for that, but for fear that that poor little body should foul our propeller when it was cast into the indifferent sea. Never can a newly married couple have had a sadder honeymoon.

But I do not want to end this talk on a note of sadness. I should like to finish by telling you of a strange and interesting character. He was an Australian, a man of fifty, who had knocked about the world all his life. He had been a soldier, a farmer, an engineer, a journalist, a baker, a professional cyclist and a tramp; could put his hand to anything, and out of the most unlikely materials make something useful. At such a time, believe me, he was a much more valuable member of society than an author or even the Governor of an Indian Province. He had found himself a cubby-hole under the fo'c'sle head to sleep in, and this after some days he invited me to share. It was tiny and smelly, for the ship's stores were kept there, and it was there the bos'n kept the cables; but we had it to ourselves. With two planks laid side by side on three baskets my friend made a long narrow bed that we could lie on end to end, and it was a luxury after the iron deck. Out of an empty jam-tin he made a convenient pail, and he taught me how easily one can have a good wash with half a pint of water. This jam-tin we used also to fetch our soup at the midday ration. He scrounged a broom from somewhere and made a shovel out of the top of a biscuit-tin, so that we were not only able to sweep the cubby-hole clean but to get rid of the dirt when we had swept it up. He had a use for every empty jam-jar and for every empty tin. Nothing could be left lying about that he didn't fix with a beady eye, and if you didn't stop him he'd start making a coat-hanger, a box, a stool or anything else in the world that occurred to him. He was the tidiest man I ever knew. I am tidy too. I put things away, but then forget where I put them. He never did. He always knew where anything was to be found, and the only thing that ever exasperated him was if you tried to find something for yourself instead of asking him to find it for you. We had no door to our cubby-hole, and it was very cold just before dawn. One night I awoke to find him putting his own blanket round me. He was angry with me when I wouldn't have it, and next day, out of a few bits of wood and a bit of sacking, he made a screen which partly covered the opening and so kept out the worst of the wind. He had owned a little house up in the hills behind Nice, and like the rest of us had been obliged to leave it and all his belongings. He had his whole fortune in his pocket. It amounted to three and sixpence. But he faced the future with fearlessness and an engaging grin.

The Rt. Hon. Isaac Foot

DRAKE'S DRUM

TODAY IS THE sixteenth of August. On the sixteenth of
August three hundred and fifty-two years ago Sir Francis
Drake and his fellow-seamen were returning from the
North Sea after putting the finishing touches to the defeat
of the Spanish Armada.

A few days ago I walked along Plymouth Hoe and
looked again—I suppose for the thousandth time—at the
statue of Sir Francis Drake. There he stands, the compass
in his hand, the globe by his side, looking out upon
Plymouth Sound and across those shining waters that
were the theatre of his mighty exploits. We West
Country folk like to think that he stands there always on
guard. A few miles away from Plymouth is Buckland
Abbey, his country home, and there is his Drum—the
Drum which he took with him round the world. A
suggestion has been made that the time interval should
be filled with the beating of Drake's Drum, and some
have said that the Drum might be taken to one of our
great National Institutions. It is more fitting that the
Drum should rest at his home, near his birthplace, and
in the very heart of the country that he loved. We in
the West Country do not need to have the sound of the
Drum brought to us over the air. We can hear it
without that help. Some of you will recall that when
in November 1918 the German Fleet surrendered and
the British Fleet, after four years of constant action and
ceaseless vigil, closed in around the enemy vessels, men
on board the Admiral's Flagship heard the long roll
of a drum. When, after careful search and inquiry,

neither drum nor drummer could be found, they realised
the truth, and by common consent one man said to
another, " Drake's Drum! "

> " *Drake he was a Devon man, an' sailed the Devon seas,*
>   *(Capten, art tha sleepin' there below ?)*
> *Rovin' tho' his death fell, he went with heart at ease,*
>   *And dreamin' arl the time o' Plymouth Hoe.*
> ' *Take my Drum to England, hang it by the shore,*
>   *Strike it when your powder's runnin' low ;*
> *If the Dons sight Devon, I'll quit the port of heaven,*
>   *And drum them up the Channel as we drummed them long*
>   *ago.* ' "

Of course, there are some matter-of-fact people who tell
us that this Drake's Drum business is only a legend, and
that in these hard days we need something more than
ghosts and legends to rely upon. Well, supposing that
we got rid of all these ghosts and legends, what then ?
Supposing we wiped out from our memory all the great
names of the past and all that we know of Drake and
Raleigh and Grenville and Blake and Nelson. What sort
of a fleet should we have left ? Surely it means something
that we give to every one of the ships in His Majesty's Navy
a *Name*. When, a few months ago, the sailors who had
fought the *Graf Spee* marched through Plymouth, the
names on their caps—*Ajax* and *Exeter*—were borne through
the streets of the city like an oriflamme. At that time
many bluejackets marched with them who bore on their
caps the name of H.M.S. *Drake*. All men belonging to
the Royal Naval Barracks in our city are reckoned to be
serving on H.M.S. *Drake*. So, whatever happens at sea,
there are always a number of our sailors who go about
" armed with that crested and prevailing name." The
name of Drake means a great deal to us now. In his
own day his very name became a terror to his enemies.
The cry of " El Draque! El Draque! " brought confusion

and panic like the descent of a fireship.   Here, in the West
Country, we are never surprised to hear the beating of
Drake's Drum.   Our fathers heard it beat when the
Mayflower made its way out of the Sound.   When Drake,
from his place upon the Hoe, watched it sail, that ship
was to him like another *Golden Hind*.

Our fathers heard it beat when Fairfax and Cromwell
came down to thank the people of Plymouth for the
defence of the town during the long siege of the Civil War.

Admiral Blake heard it when, sick unto death, he was
just able to reach the entrance to Plymouth Harbour, and
he died with his great heart lifted by the sight of the hills
of his beloved West Country and the sound of Drake's
welcoming Drum.

Nelson heard the roll of the Drum when he came to be
made a Freeman of the Borough, and Wellington heard
it, too, when he set out from Plymouth to defeat the
menace of an earlier tyranny.

The Drum was heard to beat again when Napoleon,
a prisoner after Waterloo, was brought into Plymouth
Harbour upon the *Bellerophon*.   Again and again it has
sounded during this war, especially when the troopships
have come, bringing the men of the Empire who have
travelled over those waters into which Drake was the first
to take an English keel.   The Drum was heard to beat
when we had the miracle of the deliverance of Dunkirk.
Drake's heart went out to those men who manned the
little ships that saved the British Army.   Those ships were
very much like his own—many of them were about the
same size—and they went to and fro upon the waters that
were made famous by the Battle of Gravelines when the
Invincible Armada was driven into confusion.   When we
hear the Drum, it tells us many things.   It tells first of the
confidence Drake and his fellows had in the presence of
the enemy.   He and his seamen had to fight against an
immense power—a power that seemed overwhelming—

but when they challenged that power they found it was not so strong after all, and they had a saying that Philip of Spain was a Colossus but a Colossus stuffed with clouts. Drake's seamen were like Cromwell's Ironsides: " It was ever the fashion for Cromwell's pikemen to rejoice greatly when they beheld the enemy."

The beating of the Drum also tells us of Drake's trust in the common people. He gave dignity to the common seamen, and loved to say that any boy who sailed with him would be reckoned a gentleman. He insisted that on his ship—the first English ship to plough a furrow around the world—there should be only the brotherhood of common service and sacrifice. " I must have," he said, " the gentleman to haul and draw with the mariner, and the mariner to haul and draw with the gentleman." The common sailor who sailed with Drake was raised in stature, and when the Prime Minister the other day said this was a war of the Unknown Warriors, Drake beat his Drum again. Drake had confidence in his country and confidence in the common people, but his supreme confidence was in God. " Never was fleet so strong as this," he said, as the Armada approached, " but the Lord of strength is stronger." Listen to his letter written to Walsingham at that time of national danger:

" There must be a beginning of every matter, but the continuing unto the end yields the true glory. If we can thoroughly believe that this which we do is in defence of our religion and country, no doubt our merciful God for His Christ our Saviour's sake is able and will give us the victory, though our sins be red."

Hitler, threatening invasion, reckons his forces, and tries to calculate ours. He will have to meet a good deal that is altogether beyond his reckoning and beyond his understanding. If and when he does come he will be attempting the invasion of Shakespeare's England, the land of Sir Walter Raleigh and Queen Elizabeth. They

D

will come at the sound of Drake's Drum, and others, too, like William Wallace and Robert Bruce, Owen Glendower and John Knox and Montrose.

Destitute himself of any moral greatness or spiritual resource, this mean, cruel man, standing for nothing but brute violence and proud tyrannic power, seeks to crush the land of William Tyndale and John Hampden and Oliver Cromwell and John Milton—the Britain of Marlborough (another famous Devonshireman) and John Wesley, of Chatham and Burke and Tom Paine and Charles James Fox. For the defence of this land of such dear souls, this dear, dear land, all these will rally at the sound of Drake's Drum, with Wordsworth and Burns and Shelley and Scott and Cobbett and David Livingstone and Florence Nightingale and Edith Cavell and countless others—an exceeding great army. All the old admirals will come, led by Nelson. The invader will have to meet, not only the British Navy of today, but "The Naval Reserve."

> " *Rank on rank the admirals*
> *Rally to their old commands;*
> *Where the crash of battle falls*
> *There the one-armed hero stands.*
> *Loud upon his phantom mast*
> *Speak the signals of the past.*
>
> " *Where upon the friendly wave*
> *Stand our squadrons as of old,*
> *Where the lonely deed and brave*
> *Shall the ancient torch uphold,*
> *Strive for England side by side,*
> *Those who live and those who died.*"

In this hour of grave peril and high privilege we are indeed compassed about with a great cloud of witnesses.

H. N. Brailsford

THE REBEL IN ENGLISH LITERATURE

WE ARE TALKING in this series about what England has
meant to us. What is it that we shall be defending when
Hitler's threatened invasion breaks upon our shores? A
rather startling answer came into my head when I asked
myself this question. It was this: The Englishmen whom
I have most loved and admired in my own life and in
history have all been rebels. Were they England? My
memory went back to a house built in the depths of an
oak forest. There was more in that house and round it
of the enduring changeless England than I have ever met
elsewhere. It stood on a hillock with a wide view over
the Weald of Sussex. The oak woods round it had been
fostered by the forbears of its owner as timber for the
building of Nelson's fleet. The house was of brick with a
stone roof on which a whole garden of wild flowers had
sown themselves. Innumerable nightingales added their
orchestra to the enchantment of the flowers. Over the
door were figures that dated the building of the house.
It had stood there untouched and unchanged since
Charles II was restored to his throne. No touch of
modernity spoiled its wainscoted walls. Oak logs
blazed in its open hearths. And candles lit us at night.
The only new thing I can recall within that house was a
great tapestry woven on his own looms by William Morris,
the gift of one poet to another. Behind it, I remember, a
robin used to roost. He would flutter down at meal-
times to eat out of my friend's hand. The old man to
whom this changeless fragment of England belonged

came of a long line of squires, a family so conservative
that it had refused to change its religion at the Reformation.   Through many centuries they had never given the
smallest sign of originality or even of unconventionality,
until like a changeling from another world Wilfrid Blunt
appeared to delight Victorian England with his poems
and shock it by his audacious acts of rebellion.   These old
families in Sussex had a trick of behaving in this improper
and unexpected way once in every few hundred years.
The Shelley estate lay beyond the thick oak forest where
the nightingales sang, and an old map in the hall showed
how its ancestral lands dovetailed with those of the
Blunt family.   Its long line of rather dull and respectable
squires lapsed suddenly into genius in the same way, and
the Shelley changeling, like Wilfrid Blunt, was also rebel
and poet.

A stranger or more beautiful apparition I have rarely
met in my life than this old man.   He had a tall and
active figure, with quick magnetic eyes, an aquiline nose
and a long brindled beard.   His notion of evening dress
was to don a long Arab robe of silk.   He began life in
the diplomatic service, and then, long before the journey
that made Doughty famous, he plunged with his young
wife into the wilderness of stony Arabia, over a track
that no Christian intruder had yet traversed.   His wife,
by the way, Lady Anne Blunt, came from the family of
Byron, yet another of these changeling rebels.   This
sojourn in Arabia brought to life within Wilfrid Blunt a
second self, as Byron's stay in Greece made a hero of that
noble egoist.   He learned to love the life of the desert,
its solitudes, its horses and above all its men.   He found
Islam sympathetic and learned to look on the world from
the angle of his Arab friends, whose passion was freedom.
Blunt came to manhood in our last epoch of imperial
expansion that began with the bombardment of Alex-
andria and the occupation of Egypt and culminated

in the Boer War. It was no rare thing for rebels from the middle and working class to fight this tendency. John Bright, the Quaker orator, used all his massive eloquence against our proceedings in Egypt, and half the Liberal Party of that day opposed the Boer War.

But Blunt came from the ruling class. His life was an incessant struggle, not merely against the excesses of Imperialism, but against the very idea of Empire itself. The originality of it all lay in the fact that his flesh and bones were those of the Empire builders: half of them in the governing class of his day were his cousins or at least his connections by marriage. This mutineer came from the captain's bridge. With Liberalism as a creed he never had the slightest sympathy. The intimate guests whom one met in his ancient Restoration house were Indian nationalists, Irish leaders and even English Socialists ; but he would always describe himself as an unrepentant Tory. When he was elected to the Carlton Club the Committee asked him if he was a good Tory: " Well," he answered, " I believe in the game laws." That was enough to satisfy the Club.

I could not in a short talk recount all he did to help the cause that of all others lay nearest to his heart, that of Egyptian nationalism. He spared neither time nor energy nor money. He was a little apt to think of the modern history of Egypt as a duel between Lord Cromer and himself. In this there was some pardonable exaggeration. But the episode in Blunt's life that I like to remember best was his challenge to his own Party over Ireland. He insisted on speaking at a proclaimed meeting in the days of coercion, and he had his reward. He served a sentence in Kilmainham gaol. A suit of prison clothes, adorned with the broad arrow, hung ever afterwards in his wardrobe beside the Arab robe. He would wear it in state once a year. Did he ever dine in it, I wonder, at the Carlton Club ? Blunt will live in his published diaries among the most astonishing personalities of the Victorian age. Some of his shorter poems have a sure place in every good anthology, but it is a belief of mine that one of his longer poems, " Satan Absolved," is great literature. Satan indicts to the Lord God in stately hexameters all the works of man, his cruelty to the nobler wild beasts, his massacre of the birds, his wars and his imperial conquests. This noble indignation was the man.

You all know Browning's line: " And did you once see Shelley plain ? " I almost did. He lived again in this neighbour of the same stock, a lesser poet but as bold a rebel. They had this in common. Never in a long life could they grow accustomed to wrong and oppression. Always they met it with the same wide-eyed surprise, the same fresh and fruitful anger. Shelley's rebellion, to be sure, went far deeper. It was the whole structure of society that revolted him. But he would have endorsed the whole of that terrific indictment that Blunt put into Satan's mouth, and I think he would have applauded the music of Blunt's verse.

How did they happen, these aristocratic rebels ? To me they are as English as anything in our English heritage. They were odd only because they believed more literally in our English tradition of freedom and humanity than the average men around them. If their birth in a long line of squires meant anything, it meant that England lived in them as she lived in the oaks of their estates. They knew what was great and lasting in her, and they condemned what was ephemeral and unworthy in their day. It is our oddity as a nation that if crimes and excesses stain our record, as they stain the record of every nation, the protests they evoked belong even more truly to our history. It does not greatly matter today that Warren Hastings may have robbed the princesses of Oude. But the eloquence of Burke's denunciation is part of our national heritage. Burke was no rebel as

Shelley was and Blunt and Byron were, but in that great speech and in some others he performed the duty of the rebel who defies successful and popular wrong. The saving grace of the English is that we tolerate our rebels and even listen to them with one of our ears. When there is a Charles there will always be a Hampden, and if Cromwell turns Führer a Colonel John Lilburne will arise. Cromwell ranks as the most famous of our English rebels, and Lilburne was rebel against this rebel. But the truth about Cromwell is that he was a rebel rather by reason of the circumstances of his day than by temperament. He was not a man who enjoyed rebellion—rather he did it against the grain in obedience to the imperative voice of conscience. His part in the Civil War was to introduce order and system into what was, before he took charge, a somewhat inefficient rebellion. His objects were limited. He would not suffer the autocratic rule of one man, but it was only the heroic obstinacy, if you like to call it so, of King Charles that manœuvred him into the overthrow of the monarchy.

But in everything Cromwell was a man of order. The character of the man—his physical courage, his audacity and his magnetism over men—was never seen to better advantage than when he suppressed the Leveller mutineers among the troopers of New Model at Ware, by riding boldly into their midst and seizing their emblem single-handed. But his English moderation and humanity on that occasion were as notable as his daring. For the rest, he stood for property against the Levellers, and strictly opposed their very moderate proposals for manhood suffrage subject to a good many qualifications. If Cromwell had lived in the next century he would have been a very moderate Whig. In our day he would be a rather inarticulate inhabitant of a Tory back-bench.

If in that age you seek a type of the rebel of genius a better candidate would be Cromwell's opponent and critic, the leader of the Levellers, Colonel John Lilburne. While he is still an apprentice in the City, he must organise the smuggling into London of forbidden books, secretly printed in Holland. The books would strike us today as harmless and dull, but they were forbidden fruit. Lilburne was flogged all the way from the City to Charing Cross, but as he stood in the pillory he still had strength to make a fiery speech to the crowd. After months on bread and water in a subterranean dungeon, he still had the physical vigour to fight in the Civil War to such purpose that in spite of wounds he rose in a few months to the rank of Lieut.-Colonel. How often was he tried for his life on a political charge? How often did he defy, not merely Lords and Commons, but the leaders of the victorious army as well? I like to think of him addressing a company of soldiers, sent to arrest him, on the fundamentals of English liberty with such compelling logic that they saluted and left him at large. This man was the very genius of rebellion.

But what was it all about? Something highly reasonable and law-abiding: Lilburne wanted to set out the fundamentals of our native liberties in an agreed charter. That is English rebellion.

Bernard Darwin

ONE MAN'S LIFE

IN THE ARMY at Salonika, where I was in the last war, there was an officer who was extremely tall. He said that whenever he saw strangers about to speak to him he knew exactly what they were going to say. So he had this answer ready; he remarked " Six feet ten inches " and passed on his way. I feel rather as he did because, if your name happens to be Darwin, everyone is sure to say to you: " I suppose you are scientific too ? " So I, too, have my answer ready in the words of an old friend of mine, Sir Walter Fletcher. He was a man of science and a Fellow of the Royal Society, but also an athletic blue. He said to me one day: " You know, you've got the scientific mind gone addled." I have no doubt whatever that he was right as to the second epithet: my only doubt is as to the first. Perhaps I ought, in fairness to my family, to say that they never tried to make me scientific. I expect they saw it was a hopeless job. In one respect I must have taken after my great-uncle Ras, Charles Darwin's brother. He was a charming old gentleman who was a friend of the Carlyles and used to drive Mrs. Carlyle about London in his cab. One of my earliest memories is of going to his house in Queen Anne Street. After saying my how-do-you-do's to him I was sent down to the dining-room with the butler, and there regaled on grapes of a quality so scrumptious that I have never met their like since. Uncle Ras was not scientific. When told by his brother some interesting piece of natural history he replied, " My dear fellow, I don't give a damn for the whole kingdom of Nature."

Those were and are my sentiments. As far as I was anything, I suppose I was a classical little boy—since I got a scholarship at Eton by my classics, though I didn't subsequently live up to it. With one or two exceptions, such as mine, the scientific strain has remained very strong in the family ever since the time of my great-great-grandfather Erasmus Darwin. He was a very remarkable old gentleman, and possibly the worst poet that ever lived ; certainly the worst who was ever paid a guinea a line for his verses. It continues just as strongly today, except in my own particular branch. My poor father, who was a botanist of some distinction, produced a daughter who is a poet and a very good one, my sister Frances Cornford, and a son who is, I suppose, a mildly literary gent.

Though I am constitutionally incapable of anything scientific, I think I know what Walter Fletcher meant about my unfortunate, addled mind. I had a certain power of storing things up in it. Whether quotations from my favourite books, or the names of cricketers, football players, golfers and, as an odd side-line, murderers —I could reel off their achievements and their initials with gusto and considerable accuracy. This is very far from being a great gift, but it has turned out a useful one to me. Golf liberally sprinkled with Dickens quotations has meant for me bread reasonably sprinkled with butter and even sometimes a little jam. And so I regard myself as a lucky man in having been able to do the only thing I could really have enjoyed doing. I think I always wanted to write about games. When I was a rather lonely small boy I used to invent whole imaginary Elevens with names elaborately composed out of those of the family dogs, cats or horses. I used to write them letters inviting them to play in international matches between imaginary countries. Subsequently I wrote accounts of these matches in the best sporting journalese—that now, alas! vanished

language in which the leather was planted between the
uprights and someone always trundled from the Gasworks
end. I regret something of its fine old formality and the
modest headline which used to announce in small type
" Another century by Dr. Grace." Today it seems, in my
old-fashioned view, that the main object of some writers
is not to describe the game or try even to show that they
know much about it. They often don't. What they
want is to show how well they know the players and to
refer to them all, especially the young ladies, by their
Christian names.

That, however, is an incidental and a mere senile
complaint. Writing about games did not seem a possible
occupation when I came down from Cambridge in 1897—
indeed, it was hardly then an occupation at all, and it never
occurred to me to tell my father that I should like to do it.
So I plunged, without any vast enthusiasm, into the law.
First into a solicitor's office in the city, and, when I found
that I could not abide that, into a barrister's chambers in
the Temple. In point of fact, I rather like law and always
try to get my legal friends to talk their shop to me, even
though it is not about murder; but I am afraid I did
not like it passionately enough. When I had a brief,
which was very, very seldom, the summit of my ambition
was not to make too big a fool of myself, and my real long-
ing was for Saturday to come round again, and bring me
my week-end's golf at Woking. I played a good deal of
golf, especially on summer evenings when one could
sneak away to Chiswick or Richmond a little early and
get a round, even without daylight saving. I generally
managed to get to the Championship Meeting, but I was
not wholly without virtue. I missed two of them altogether, and another time I went all the way to Scotland for
two nights just for the international match, was severely
defeated and returned limp and dejected to Chambers.

I am afraid I was too often looking over the edge of my

work for my play to begin, and that is not a good plan.   I
did write one or two casual articles for casual guineas at
long intervals, but I never seriously thought of doing more
until suddenly, as it seemed by a miracle, there came a
chance of doing a regular weekly one.   Then, by another
miracle—a stray meeting with Lord Riddell in the corridor
of the Law Courts—there came a second chance.   I was
after it like a shot from a gun, sold my wig, which was
suspiciously clean, walked out of the Temple for ever, and
into Fleet Street next door.

. No doubt I was lucky in my opportunity—it came at
the right time.   The newspapers had then only lately
tumbled to the fact that people liked to read about games,
liked it at least as well, for instance, as interminable reports
of parliamentary debates or stodgy leaders about them.
A little while before I began to write golf in *The Times*, all
the games, of whatever kind, in that great journal were
reported by one and the same man.   His name was Ward,
and he was called Sporting Ward to distinguish him from
the eminent Mr. Humphry Ward, who wrote on
pictures.   At any rate, having got the two jobs to write
about golf, I quickly got another and yet another, till I
had to cut them down to two in all.   Those two I have,
except for war-times, been doing steadily since 1908.
What is more, I have never got tired of it, and I hope some
happy day to be hard at it again.   E. V. Lucas once gave
me a book of his with a very kind inscription beginning
" To Bernard Darwin who has kept his eye on the wrong
ball."   Well, perhaps I have, but it is a great stand-by in
journalism to have one ball of whatever kind, one subject
that you are supposed, even if quite wrongly, to know
something about.   It has its disadvantages, too, of course.
When a few years ago I was Captain of the Royal and
Ancient Golf Club of St. Andrews, a friend of mine over-
heard a conversation between two old ladies on the ladies'
putting green.   The ladies are interested in the Captain

because he gives them a prize. One of them said: " Do you know who the new Captain is ? " The other replied: " I believe he's a kind of journalist. I *think* his name is Garvin." She did me too much honour. I certainly was not that illustrious gentleman and I have never tried to write about politics, but I have written about a good many odds and ends of things besides golf—and the depressing thing is that very few people will ever believe it. That is apt to happen to those who are supposed to do one thing. I have always felt rather sorry for certain artists. They get a small reputation for painting, let us say, cows browsing in a green field or, perhaps, cavaliers riding under a castle gate. People never imagine that the poor man would like to paint something else now and then, and they probably won't buy his picture if he does. He is just labelled " the cow man," and that's that. I get rather tired, as I said, of polite persons who ask, " Are you scientific too ? " But I get still more tired of those who ask, " Why don't you write about something else besides golf ? "

You must not think that I am ungrateful or in the very least ashamed of writing about golf. I am prepared to cross swords with anyone on behalf of sporting writers. Some people seem to think of them as all sunk in the same abyss, utterly outside the pale. That only shows how stupid these people are and how ignorant of good literature, because there is magnificent writing about sport. Just think for a moment of Borrow and Hazlitt about prize fighting. Is there anything more spirited and racy in the English language than Hazlitt's essay called " The Fight," or his truly noble account of Cavanagh the Fives Player ? Think of the Druid on Hunting, and some of Dick Christian's lectures; or Tom Hughes's account of the School House match in *Tom Brown's Schooldays*. And what richness there is in the literature of cricket! It begins with John Nyren and the early heroes of Hambledon, and comes right down to the present day, with the late Mr. Bob Lyttelton's description of Cobden's over, or Mr. Neville Cardus growing lyrical over Johnny Tyldesley at Old Trafford.   At any rate, we who come after—very far after, faint and pursuing—have as good models to follow as anyone can desire, writing that anyone, yes anyone, might envy.   And with that little outburst I come to an end of this, I am afraid, egotistical talk.   Looking back, I've spent much of my time in green and pleasant places, and with pleasant people, doing the thing I liked.   It's been good fun.   I am unrepentant and very, very far from ungrateful.

E. V. Knox

"PUNCH"

I HAVE A cutting from an Irish paper which says, " *Punch* has now been going for a hundred years and has hardly let one of those years go by without making a joke of one sort or another." Perhaps the writer exaggerates. Anyhow, it is only the beginning of August, so we have plenty of time still to get our joke ready for this year if we can think of one. You won't get it tonight. I am only here to say a few words about the way *Punch* began, and possibly to explain why it still goes on, in spite of that difficulty of finding a new joke every fifteen months or so.

I think the paper is best known to most people for the drawings of John Leech, Charles Keene, George du Maurier and Phil May, and later artists, some still living, of whom every reader probably has his or her own favourite—and one or two not so favourite. I think they're all very good. Later reputations are no doubt less clearly fixed, but from 1841 till now the artists have all been using every sort of burlesque or mildly comic style to represent or make fun of British manners, customs, fashions and institutions, from Parliament at Westminster to porters at Covent Garden, from drawing-rooms in Mayfair (whatever that is) to gatherings round the village pump or inside the village inn. There have also been a good number of well-known writers from Thackeray and Anstey down to the present time, and they also have tried to represent in prose and verse the social and political scene with different sorts of fun. Sometimes they mocked, sometimes they raged (like Hood with his " Song of the

Shirt "), sometimes they merely recorded lightly the social scene.

At the beginning they raged. They were violent social reformers. Later they became milder. If there are many centenarians listening to me (and I hope there are a lot), they will perhaps forgive Mr. Punch for being more hot-headed in his early youth than he is today. The reason is partly, I think, that the kind of abuses that he used to attack (like sweated labour) are not so common as they were. Nor do I think that even those bygone reformers in *Punch* made themselves very uncomfortable in the cause for which they stood. Leech liked hunting. " Give me a good day's hunting and plenty of good claret after it, and I'm quite content," he said at one of the Round Table dinners.

When I look back at the old Victorian scene presented in *Punch*, it seems to me, through the mist of years, a panorama of crinolines and queer bathing dresses, of gentlemen clinging to lamp-posts, and sporting adventures by flood and field. When I think of Leech the words that stick in my head are the words under a picture of a groom looking at a horse that has been both ridden and driven. " It isn't the 'unting as 'urts 'im, it's the 'ammer, 'ammer along the 'ard 'igh road." When I think of Charles Keene, I remember the gentleman coming back very late at night. " What do you mean by coming home at this time ? " his wife says to him. " Sorry, my dear," he answers, " all the other places shur-rup." Not that either of the pictures represents the best work of Leech (who drew everything) or of Keene (who was incomparably the best artist it has ever been the good fortune of Mr. Punch to secure). It is merely that these are the familiar and constantly recurring subjects of the old *Punches* of those old days. Later, when we come to George du Maurier, *Punch* seems to have advanced very much into the drawing-rooms, to be always chatting with formidable hostesses, to be intimate with musicians and artists and ambassadors, to be strolling in the Park, to be very contemptuous of anyone who has recently made his money in trade. Very long descriptions of every scene are written underneath. It is a favourite theory of one of my colleagues that these long descriptions, ending with such phrases as " sensation " or " collapse of the unfortunate Archdeacon," were sent to *Punch* by contributors, sent back unchanged by the Editor to the artists, sent back again unchanged to the Editor, and sent finally still unaltered to the printer. Happy days. But Phil May, who was born in Leeds but worked for a year or two with the *Sydney Bulletin*, like my friend Mr. Low, the famous cartoonist of the *Evening Standard*, takes us right into the streets and the humours of coster life and 'Appy 'Arry on 'Ampstead Bank Holidays.

I'm not going to talk about more recent contributors and writers. There are so many of them, and some have been so good. Listeners who know the paper will not need me to tell them whom they ought to like best.

But there is quite a different side to *Punch*. The people who started it meant it to have a serious side, not only for matters at home, but also for matters abroad. *Punch* in the puppet show has a big stick and *Punch* as a paper intended to use it when he felt inclined. The first Editor was Mark Lemon, and he remained as Editor for nearly thirty years. When there was still a doubt as to whether *Punch* was a good name for the paper one of the founders was asked, " What would punch be without lemon ? Let's call it *Punch*." That was the joke for 1841, I suppose. You couldn't make it now because we haven't any lemons. This just shows how humour alters in the course of the years. The present cover (not the first that was tried) was drawn by Richard Doyle, and he gave an indication of the political side of the paper by showing Mr. Punch with a pen in his hand having just made a sketch of a lion's

E

head. The head, in fact, of the British lion. Doyle and
Leech were the first cartoonists.

Punch invented the word cartoon as applied to political
pictures or caricatures and not used in the ordinary sense
in which artists use the word, which is as a model for a
large wall painting. This was because in 1843 there was
a great exhibition of the cartoons for the historical paintings in Westminster Hall. Mr. Punch, professing himself
also to be a serious artist, said that he would also exhibit
cartoons in his new paper, and thus began the ordinary
second sense of the word. From the start the cartoon side
of *Punch* was considered to be very important, and it was
to settle these " cuts " or cartoons that the staff met, and
has continued to meet, at the original Round Table, on
which they carved and still carve their initials. It was the
supreme good luck of *Punch* that after Leech died, Tenniel
became cartoonist and drew cartoons for forty years.
There was, of course, nothing of the kind in daily papers
then, and Tenniel's caricatures of the political figures of
his day made him a power in the land, and he had good
successors in Linley Sambourne and Sir Bernard Part-
ridge.

None of them has ever forgotten the British lion that
Doyle drew on the cover. What a lot of work it has done
for us ! Animals in cartoons are good or bad or doubtful
animals. Tigers are bad ; elephants are usually good ;
wolves and jackals, of course, are bad ; bears and eagles
are doubtful ; camels, which are only used at Budget
times, are merely patient ; snakes and dragons are very
bad indeed. Snakes and dragons (one must admit) are
accommodating as well as bad. Being very long, they
can have long words like totalitarian written in capital
letters along them, so that nobody can mistake what you
mean. You can't write totalitarianism on a lion, even
if you want to, which you don't. Except for moments
of laziness and apathy, this British lion is always noble,

always good. Leech in 1848 drew a very fat and very
complacent British lion with a sailor's hat on being
admonished by the Duke of Wellington. There was then
a scare of invasion. Tenniel drew another lazy lion
being prodded by Disraeli and John Bright. That was
about the Reform Bill in 1859. Sometimes this cartoon
lion would get on his hind legs and roar or would go to
sea, or carry a bayonet to show he was willing to defend
the Empire or the cliffs of Dover. Sometimes he hands
over his job to St. George or John Bull. I don't think
all three of them ever appear together in one cartoon.
Between 1841 and 1888 I have counted, I think, thirty
appearances of the British lion. Once he is smelling a
rat. That was at the Peace Conference in Paris in 1886.
The cartoon in 1888 is called " The German Fox and the
British Lion." Foxes in cartoons are always bad.
Sometimes in former days the British lion had cubs
around him. They would bear the names of Colonies.
But several of them grew up and became Dominions,
and one of them, in any case, was always changing into a
kangaroo and playing cricket with this cartoon lion.
Kangaroos in cartoons are always good, even when they
win too easily. Naturally in war-time the lion becomes
more serious, more dignified. Last year he had to be
shown standing at bay with a spear in his side. That
was Dunkirk. His very latest appearance was most
unusual and most unorthodox. He had changed clothes
with a bear. He had put on the Russian cap and big
boots, and the bear had put on the hat of John Bull and
his tail-coat and his old-school tie. That was because
they were both going hunting together—hunting snakes
perhaps in a wood. *Punch*, indeed, has been so much
indebted all through these hundred years to that lion on
Richard Doyle's cover, and drawn him in so many
positions and places, and so many suits of clothes, that
the present staff of the Round Table thought the least

they could do would be to adopt a lion at the Zoological Gardens for the duration of this war. Strangely enough, he is an Abyssinian lion, and doing nicely, thank you ! If he were as obliging as the Hollywood lion, I have no doubt I should have been able to let you hear him roar. The best thing about a lion is that he doesn't need a joke to make him roar.

W. SOMERSET MAUGHAM

SIR PHILIP GIBBS

Sir Philip Gibbs

WAR CORRESPONDENTS PAST
AND PRESENT

THE VIVID DESPATCHES from the war fronts by Richard
Dimbleby, Edward Ward, and others have aroused some
discussion and curiosity about the work of war correspondents and how it compares with that of their predecessors. Doubtless our present chroniclers of war have
lost some of the romantic glamour of those who went
before them. Military control and strict censorship are
apt to cramp one's style and restrict one's liberty of
personal adventure. The old war correspondents of the
Victorian era—which provided many little wars to keep
them busy—were professional adventurers who interested
the public in their own personality and exploits. Among
them were such gallant fellows as Archibald Forbes,
Bennett Burleigh, Frederick Villiers, Charlie Hands, and
my old friend Henry Nevinson—the last and noblest of
that band, now over eighty and annoyed with fate which
prevents him from going to the Front again in the present
war. . . . They were deadly rivals—these old-time war
correspondents. They did desperate deeds to get the
news first to their own papers. Some of them were
pretty ruthless in their rivalry, and one of them, as I was
told, threw another man's kit out of the baggage van in
order to hold him up on his journey. They raced across
deserts on horse or camel to get first to a telegraph line.
The hire of camels was a frequent item on their expenses
accounts and covered a multitude of drinks. Some
of them dressed the part, and old Frederick Villiers,
whom I encountered in the first phase of the last war,

used to appear on the lecture platform in a slouch hat and riding breeches, with a pistol and knife in his belt, looking ready to start that very moment for the next battle.

I was a late comer to their ranks and a mere novice. My first campaign was in the Balkan Wars of 1912–13, and I had a thin time. I had not been in Belgrade more than two hours before I was taken for an Austrian spy and marched through the streets to the nearest lock-up. That was a bad beginning, and things didn't go well from first to last. We were not allowed army rations and food was scarce. I remember lounging about with two companions outside the mess of the military attachés in order to sniff the succulent smell of their baked meats. A horde of correspondents came from all countries, spoiling the game by their numbers and alarming the armies to which they were accredited. An iron censorship was established, and we were treated more like prisoners of war than friendly observers.

This new hostility to the war correspondents was shared by Lord Kitchener, and also by French generals when the first world war began in 1914. For many months permission was refused for correspondents to accompany our expeditionary force. Some of us, however, took a chance and went out to France before the first shot was fired. I was one of them, and with two companions— H. M. Tomlinson, the famous writer, and Massey of the *Daily Telegraph*—had amazing adventures in the early months of the war. One of our little troubles was to know exactly where the enemy might be—it's always well to know—and several times we had narrow escapes. Hamilton Fyfe of the *Daily Mail* was taken by a cavalry patrol, but they were too busy to bother about him and he got away. I went into Belgium, and saw the retreat from Antwerp and many tragic scenes. I was in Dixmude when it was on fire and defended by the French *fusilier marins*, who were hard pressed. In the town hall only one French officer stood alive among many dead comrades. I was in the retreat from Mons in those early months. I saw enough of war to last me a lifetime. But there were four more years to come.

I was in the bad books of the War Office for this freelance work. In fact, I was down for arrest at every port in France. At Le Havre I was " pinched " by Scotland Yard detectives with commissioned rank and taken before a very fierce general who threatened to have me shot against a white wall. I was not unduly alarmed, not believing that I should face a firing squad. I was kept under arrest for ten days or so, and had time to reflect that my short career as a war correspondent had come to an end. Oddly enough, a few weeks later I was chosen to be one of the seven official correspondents accredited to the British Army in France.

At first we had a difficult time. We were put into a uniform without officer's badges, but with the green arm band of the Intelligence Corps. We had to break down a suspicion that we were dirty dogs who would probably give away information to the enemy by our newspaper articles. We seven men had five censors who lived, ate, and slept with us and conducted us to the trenches or various headquarters. By degrees we smashed this prejudice against us, and the censors became our friends and comrades. They were a charming group of men, to whom we became devoted. One of them was C. E. Montague, the famous novelist and journalist. Another was a romantic character named Faunthorpe, an Indian cavalry officer who had killed eighty-two tigers and written several sonnets. He wore a monocle, through which he regarded life and war with humorous cynicism. The general and battalion officers came to know and trust us. But prejudices lingered in the mind of Sir Douglas Haig, and when he became Commander-in-Chief he made certain regulations which would have handicapped us severely. We requested an interview which he granted, and his first words were discouraging and humiliating. He could not understand what useful purpose we were serving. After all, he said, we were only writing for Mary Ann in the kitchen. He was surprised by the heat of our answers. I was surprised by my own eloquence. We pointed out to him that war could not be fought as a secret affair, and that the nation would not stand for the sacrifice of its men without knowing what they were doing with more detail than was given in the dry lines of official despatches. Their daily heroism deserved all the record we could give them. Haig altered his mind on the spot and with complete generosity. He withdrew all restrictions and gave us more facilities than any war correspondents had ever had. He allowed us to visit any part of the line at any time. He gave us the right of access to all reports from the army down to battalion headquarters during the course of any action. Beach Thomas and I wrote some of the Commander-in-Chief's weekly reports at his own request.

We made friends with most of the generals and battalion officers, and our narratives of the battles were accurate and full, for we saw the war during those years at close range and with all available information before us. Our reading public fretted, and cursed us no doubt, because the censorship did not allow us often to mention individual units in which their sons were serving. I still believe that rule to have been a mistake, at least when the enemy knew what men were against them, as mostly they did. It was also believed that we were " spoon-fed " by official dope. That was because we all told the same story with the same incidents, in different style. That was inevitable and not, in my opinion, objectionable. We decided ourselves that this war was too big for personal rivalry or " scoops " and that our job was to record its action day by day as far as we could gather all details into the fullest possible narrative.   During a battle we used to separate and go to different parts of the line and visit different headquarters for the latest reports. In the evening we made a rendezvous and pooled this information, keeping nothing back but our personal experiences and impressions.   Our despatches—running into columns day by day when big battles were in progress—were censored on the spot by those comrades of ours who had been with us everywhere.   Often there were not more than a few lines cut, and then they were taken by despatch riders to G.H.Q. from which they were wired to the War Office.   After leaving the field, they were not allowed to be cut or altered by any word.

We seven men covered the whole English-speaking world.   Our articles were distributed throughout the Press in this country and the Dominions, as well as the United States when they came into the. war.

We saw the whole sweep and fury of the war on the Western Front during those four years.   It was often a heart-breaking job and wearing to the nerves.   We were perhaps more sensitive to its tragedy than fighting soldiers, being lookers-on, though we took some of the risks and walked often in sinister places under the menace of death ; not health resorts, as we used to say.   Young battalion officers used to put our courage to the test by taking us to their most dangerous parts of the lines, and we tried to look brave, which is the next best thing to being brave, though a great strain at times.   " Just in time to see a mine blown up," said a cheery general, fingering a telephone message.   Down in the mine shaft we could hear through a microphone the enemy coughing and spitting and getting deeper towards our gallery.   " We may be blown up at any moment," said a tunnelling officer. " It is not amusing."   I was not amused.

Clemence Dane

OUR BIBLE

YOU KNOW, BRITAIN is an extraordinarily permanent country. Last week-end I drove past my old home in Kent, and, slowing down to look at it, I wondered to see that it was quite unchanged in the forty years, although it lies not twenty-five miles from the heart of London. One still drove to it through cloth-of-gold fields—England is all buttercups this week—the deer were still grazing in the park opposite, and the little paths on to the common trekked round the same heavy-laden pink and white may trees. The only difference was the hedges, green instead of white with dust, because nowadays they asphalt the roads. The house itself looked as if my father and my dog Gip would come out the next moment through the open door, and on the lawn there still stood the huge cedar of Lebanon, a black velvet romance against the summer sky.

Then I remembered something. I remembered the hot June morning thirty-eight years ago, when we all sat out under the same cedar waiting for " news of the King." Edward VII's coronation had been put off because of his sudden illness, and the whole business of England had stopped until we knew for certain if he would live or die— for he was loved.

It was the first time I had ever experienced such tension. I did not know it again till those three August days in 1914. Today one knows it hourly, with wonder that our universe can be so shaken, yet curiously enough with no sense of dismay, but merely with intensification of all one's personal and racial memories.

What is Britain, to mean so much to us ? And to

what can we point and say: Look! This is her symbol;
this is the thing we can't afford to lose. Is it Westminster
Abbey? But York and Canterbury would have a word
to say to that. London? There is always Edinburgh.
Shakespeare? There is Chaucer—there is Burns. The
Cotswolds? There is Snowdon. The rose? But there's
also the thistle and the leek. What is the true history
and mirror of ourselves?

I think the answer is " the English Bible ! "

Of course it is just like us to be represented by something in essence remote, so like us to take as " typically
English " the cedar of Lebanon, to think of it only as the
centre of an English lawn, with a tea-table, dogs, tennis,
and a piano practising " one—two—three—four—five "
in the distance, and never to remember that the cedar
is the noblest tree of the East.

An ancient Greek wrote of it: " The wood is ever-
lasting, and therefore the images of the gods are made
from it." In India they call it the deodar, the god-tree.
And this tree of life, this god-tree, our ancient English
Bible, came to us first from that persecuted people of the
East whose battles we fight today. Our Old Testament is
the Holy Law of the Jews, and our New Testament—but
you know how the new branch sprang from the old tree,
how, to our Christian thinking, the Prince of Peace gave
us the new law which today we are struggling to vindicate.

He came—He went. Within a few years His followers
began to write down all that they could remember con-
cerning Him. But it was not till the middle of the fourth
century that St. Jerome compiled from all their writings
and letters, from the Greek manuscripts and Hebrew
texts, the great Bible which, for a thousand years, was the
basis of the Scriptures in the West. But it was written in
Latin. The first person to retell bits of it in our tongue
was a Northumbrian cowherd called Caedmon, who lived
nearly thirteen hundred years ago. It was the custom in

his days for people to improvise songs when they met at a
feast. But it was too difficult for Caedmon, and he used to
slip off to his stable early in the evening rather than be
laughed at. One snowy night as he lay among his cattle
fretting over his ignorance, he saw a vision of Christ,
Who bade him: " Sing Me a song! " and Caedmon woke
to find himself chanting:

> " *Now must we praise*
> *The grandeur of Heaven's kingdom,*
> *The creator's might*
> *And His mind's thought.*"

He had become a poet overnight.

He carried his story to Hilda the Abbess, and she translated for him tale after tale from St. Jerome's Bible, and
these he turned into native verse. And after his death
his story was written down by our first English historian,
Bede, and a few years later translated back again into
English by King Alfred himself. Admit that you can't
find a more British picture, even today, than this of a
farm labourer and a scholar and a king following up each
other's work in order to give the country something it
needed!

Caedmon, Bede, Alfred—these three planted the god-
tree in our soil, and at once its roots struck deep; but it
could not grow quickly because our language was only in
the making. The spirit had to wait upon the word.
Besides, in less than two hundred years after Alfred's
death, Britain was overwhelmed by the Normans, and our
ancient manuscripts were treated much as the Czechs
were treated this winter in Prague. Centuries had to
pass before the speech of the conquerors and the con-
quered fused into plain English. But by the end of the
fourteenth century Crécy had been fought, the poet
Chaucer was writing the " Canterbury Tales," and the
English people had been given their first true English
Bible. John Wycliffe made it.

Imagine what that book must have meant to our fathers ! We British people have always loved stories. I suppose we and the Americans read more novels today than any other peoples in the world, and here was suddenly a library of the East made wholly ours; for Wycliffe somehow manages to write as if Palestine were England. The Sea of Galilee might be Windermere, and the river Jordan becomes uncommonly like our own river Thames. Take one passage as an example. He wants to translate the wonderful parable beginning: " Consider the lilies of the field, how they grow " ; but one feels that he is trying to make his readers imagine, not the anemones of Palestine, but their own buttercups and daisies. In it he says: " If God clothith thus the *hei of the field*." And when, nearly two hundred years later, his Bible, surviving all attempts to destroy it, flowers again in Tyndale's magnificent version, it has become: " Wherefore if God so clothed the *grasse* . . ."

Tyndale's Bible was published when the whole of Europe was suffering the birth pangs of Reformation, and Tyndale was filled with the passionate desire that everyone, from King Henry VIII on his throne to the boy that drives the plough, should know the national book. And only three years after he died at the stake, crying with his last breath, " Lord, open the King of England's eyes! " his prayer was answered, and the Bible was installed in every parish church in the country.

For nearly a century the English genius continued to work on its national book. Coverdale's, Matthew's, and the Great Bible appeared in turn. The five years' torment under Mary passed and Queen Elizabeth pauses in Cheapside to kiss an English Bible and thank her city for the best of all its offerings. Finally our first Scottish King, James, a man of singular wisdoms as well as singular follies, set the scholars to work once more, and the result was the Authorised Version. Magna Carta 1215—the

Authorised Version 1611: between these two events lies the making of a nation's character and the ripening of a nation's soul. In those years the English people had realised their own destiny, had decided what virtues they most loved, what sins they most hated, and embodied their law and their speech in their Bible.

And then a strange thing came about. From that moment the Bible took charge, preserving in turn English character and English speech. It was the one book, through all the ensuing centuries, that everybody read. Fashions in literature grew and died, but the Bible knew no decay. It remained the liberal education of every English-speaking man and woman until our own times.

It is a tragedy that Bible-reading is declining. I am not speaking from the point of view of any religion, but purely as one believing that today any British child who is brought up on the Bible has a better chance to survive, and to help his island to survive, than the child who has missed such training. Take away certain physical foods from a child and it gets rickets. Take away certain mental foods from a child and its character suffers an impoverishment that no later reading or thinking can quite make good. Our sloppy modern speech, our sloppy modern mass-thinking, need discipline. But that discipline can only come, not from the learned, not from the literary, but from the people, the labouring folk who work daily in the earth of England, for they still hold by the old speech and the old ways. I had proof of that only yesterday. The gardener at home fought all through the last war, but he has gone back to the army and is now in South Africa. His wife showed me yesterday his last letter to her, asking after his two grown daughters and his little son, giving what news he could, worrying over some neglected ploughing, and ending with love and kisses. And then, after his signature, he has added a postscript. In that heavy hand, so much more accustomed to a spade than to a pen, he has written: " So be of good cheer, my dear ones! "

And I thought, as I read that postscript, of Wycliffe, six hundred years ago, writing: " Triste ye. I am. Nyle ze drede! " and of Tyndale reshaping it, two hundred years later, to: " Be of good chere! Be not a frayed! " Of Coverdale changing it to: " Be of good comfort! " And then, three reigns later, the message is authorised and confirmed to us for ever—" Be of good cheer! It is I. Be not afraid."

And that " Be of good cheer! " has echoed on down the centuries, so that today an English working-man can still use it, and so become the voice of the whole Island speaking to all the British world. It is the voice of Caedmon, the voice of Alfred, Wycliffe, Tyndale, Elizabeth, Cromwell, Nelson, Gordon—all the countless known and unknown men and women who made, who are, Britain. And the message still runs—" Be of good cheer, my dear ones! "

Hector Bolitho

SLANG

TO ME, A MAN who turns up his nose at slang is a prig. Slang brings vitality into our language, and it should be encouraged. Could there be any more lively division of the human race than in America, where you are either a *swell* guy or a *lousy* guy ? To me, that seems quite final.

Thieves have always had their slang, whether they were the narks and pimps of Hogarth's time or the hard-boiled bootleggers of the Bowery, with their gats, their molls and their hooch.

The slang of the Cockney is, of course, a precious part of our language.

Mariners have their slang—the Navy and the Army—*and the Royal Air Force*. This Air Force vocabulary of slang is already quite old—twenty years or more—and words like joy-sticks, ace, hedge-hopping, stall and zoom, born in the last war, are now accepted by the most conservative writers.

But perhaps the most interesting and best-known slang word which has come out of the Air Force is *Blimp*. Colonel Blimp has almost taken the place of John Bull, and the cartoons drawn by David Low, who, as you know, was born in New Zealand, depend for many of their laughs on the fat, moustached, downright figure of the Colonel.

I happen to know the origin of this word. It goes back to the winter of 1914 when Horace Short, the well-known aircraft designer, was standing on the steps of the Officers' Mess at Eastchurch. A violent storm was threatening just as three small airships flew low over the aerodrome. They seemed to be in a hurry to avoid the storm, and, rippling and rather limp, they floundered lower and lower. Somebody standing next to Short said, " It is ridiculous to call these things airships. Why don't you coin a name for them ? " At that moment Short called the mess waiter and asked for a " blunch," his own word, used to describe a drink half-way between breakfast and lunch. Hearing the word *blunch*, one of the officers looked up at the *limp* airships and said, " Let's call them *b*limps." So the word came into being, and now it is to be found in the most respectable dictionaries.

The word *crash* is also old. It was first used by Pay-master-Lieutenant Lidderdale in 1914. What is so curious is that we accept the word, now, quite seriously to describe an accident on landing. Twenty-six years ago it was considered witty, and it even provoked laughter.

Many of the squadrons in the Air Force have their own slang words, and a stranger in the mess could hear conversation going on without understanding a word of it. How could he know, when he heard a young pilot-officer say that he was *browned-off*, that he meant that he was depressed, or fed-up. And he might well fail to understand somebody saying, " I saw a wizard job in the village this morning." How could he suspect that the pilot-officer meant that he had seen a beautiful girl ? There are even class distinctions in the use of slang in the Service, and the fitters and riggers and other members of the ground staff frequently refer to aircraft as *kites*. They will say, " You sort of become attached to the kite on which you are working, just like a groom with his horse." The pilot himself scorns the word *kite*. *He* prefers *aircraft*.

I went to a station on the east coast a few weeks ago and talked to a rigger who was the wag of the squadron. Let me repeat a piece of his conversation. He said,

F

" I was a bit browned-off when we were stationed at X. But when we moved to Y, there were bags of excitement. The first day our kites took off to intercept some Germans." He went on, " When the raid was over we felt a bit browned-off because we were hungry, so we found a chicken and I borrowed the grid—you know, the boot scraper—from the doorstep and four of us cooked it over a fire. It took three and a half hours to cook, but it was wizard when it was finished." Most expressive ! You can almost smell that chicken !

A good deal of sailor's slang still survives in the Service, left over from the early days when there was a Royal Naval Air Service, before the Air Force was formed. The Navy are very conservative, and they brought their own words inland to Cranwell, in the heart of Lincolnshire. These sailors would not relent. They always asked for leave to " go ashore " when they wished to go into Nottingham to dine. I remember an old pilot telling me that when the grass before the officers' mess needed mowing, the N.C.O.—an old sailor—came up to him and asked if the " lawn on the *quarter-deck* could be cut." One good sailor's word you will find in the Air Force is *banger*, a sausage. That is graphic enough. I had a friend, as gay an Irishman as ever lived. He was killed a month or so ago. He was in the Air Force and used to come over to my house in Essex and cook himself sausages when he had a few hours off. One evening he called out to me, " The bangers are coming up like nobes." I had to ask before I understood that the bangers . . . the *sausages*, were coming up like *nobes* . . . like *nobody's business*.

But why the balloon squadrons use naval words for commands is more than I can understand. The square of concrete above which the balloon hangs is called the *deck*, no matter if it is in the middle of a London square. And the balloon crews go so far as to say that they want the *leave tender*, when it is the lorry they are waiting for.

Most of the everyday slang words of the Air Force are very descriptive. When a man is making a fuss, they say he is " getting into a flap," or that he is " flapping." The ornate gold oak leaves on the peak of an Air Commodore's hat are called *scrambled* eggs—quite good. I like very much their phrase to describe their attitude towards anything of which they disapprove. They say, " I take a poor view of that." A glaring error is a " black." " I have put up a black," they will say. But one of the best is used to describe some problem which they have mastered. They say, " I have got that buttoned up." There is one phrase, most descriptive, but with an origin I have never been able to trace. When a senior officer reprimands his junior, the culprit says, " He tore a strip off me." There you have the full value of slang. However obscure the origin of the phrase, I can imagine nothing which could better describe one's state of mind after being harangued by one's betters —a strip torn off.

I came upon one fascinating piece of slang a few weeks ago, when I was with some pilots in Essex. One of them said, " Oh, I'm only the ' can back king '! "

Let us work this one out. The man who has to carry the empty can back from any job is doing a rather humble task. This pilot felt that he was being put upon by his friends—made to carry the empty can back—nobody carried back as many cans as he did—so he complained that he was the *can back king*.

One good description of a man who is fussing more than necessary—harassed by what he is doing—is " a flat spin." He is in a *flat spin*. To those who know about flying, that is perfect. He is out of control, and he sees no chance of coming back into control again. And we hear also of " a Balbao " coming to England. Cast your minds back! The first pilot to lead a big formation across the Atlantic was Balbao ; the inference is obvious—a big enemy formation of aircraft coming over this country is a Balbao.

The Royal Air Force also falls in love with words and makes them fashionable for a time. Like a flash, the phrase *wicked enemy* has swept through the Service. " I met the wicked enemy." " I wonder if the wicked enemy will arrive to-night." " The wicked enemy appeared out of the clouds." It seems to be a very mild adjective, but you will hear it used, at the moment, in almost every station in the country. In a month's time it may be forgotten, and another adjective will take its place.

In the Air Ministry, of course, we use very little slang. But we have one phrase which is very descriptive. If we put an idea up to those above us and have it rejected, we say, " My idea has been shot down! " In the last war they used to say, " My idea has been torpedoed! "

I could go on with these tales for a long time. A Service which lives so vitally naturally needs original phrases with which to express itself.

So I will end by wishing you bags of luck, with the hope that you won't get into a flap or have a strip torn off you—that, in short, everything will be wizard for you for ever.

Lord Elton

BRITISH EDUCATION AND BRITISH CHARACTER

FROM THE DAWN of its history this has been a country in which men have preferred to do things for themselves. As far as possible, they wanted their rulers to leave them alone. Very early in their story they were boasting that " an Englishman's home is his castle," and long before other nations, they forced their rulers to abolish the odious right of imprisonment without trial. Within a man's own home—provided of course that he observed the law— he was to be left alone to manage his family life as he pleased. A little later this instinct for independence and for individual enterprise—the instinct which gave us the Elizabethan sea-adventurers and the Pilgrim Fathers— began to look farther afield. Men felt that it was not sufficient to be left alone by the Government. They wanted to do its work for it. They began to organise themselves into voluntary associations to work for social and political reforms which in almost every other country at that time were thought of as being the business of the State, which is another way of saying that they were neglected altogether. Thus the slave trade, and a little later slavery, among the negroes in the British colonies were abolished, much earlier than elsewhere, after a long agitation conducted by a group of private citizens led by William Wilberforce. And to-day, although the power of the State has grown so fast and so far, everyone who knows Britain knows that it is still a network of voluntary associations, trade unions, friendly societies, religious and political organisations, literary, scientific and sports

85

clubs innumerable, so that every aspect of the national life is enriched and vitalised by the free, voluntary enterprise of men and women who are not told what to do and how to think by uniformed officials, but of their own goodwill and on their own initiative contribute to the national life.   A number of these associations—the Boy Scouts and the Salvation Army, for example—have been copied all over the world.   This hereditary instinct for voluntary enterprise, this aversion from rigid dictation by the State, you will find powerfully reflected in the history of our schools.

Another deep-seated characteristic, which has intimately affected British education, is what may perhaps be called the national respect for character.   Which matters most, brains or character ?   That has always been one of the fundamental problems of education.   Some countries have always valued brains above character.   If they could have a professor to govern them they have felt that all was well.   They like their politicians " cute." " There are no flies on him," they say admiringly of their favourites.   The Englishman tends rather to say of the leader he trusts, " He's a *sound* man."   He wants intelligence in his rulers, but he profoundly mistrusts intelligence unless it is rooted in character.   Cecil Rhodes was expressing the inherited instincts of his fellow country-men when, in founding his Rhodes Scholarships, he laid it down that his scholars were to be chosen for both brains and character.   This mistrust of mere cleverness, this belief that without character—courage, resolution, unselfishness—brilliant intelligence may be not only use-less but even dangerous, is akin to that constant mistrust of abstract theory divorced from political experience which has been so constant a feature of our history. You may expect to find it plainly reflected in our schools.

A third characteristic which has moulded our education is a certain instinct for decency.   We may not be a deeply

religious people, although there can be no doubt that the
Churches have had, and still have, a most powerful
influence on national life.   But the moral code which
grew originally out of the Christian faith is deeply
ingrained in the nation, even in those members of it
who would not acknowledge membership of any Church,
or even perhaps belief in any religious creed.   British
fighting-men would not be able to bring themselves to
machine-gun refugees or life-boat crews.   They would
doubtless merely say that to machine-gun refugees would
" be unsporting " or that it was a " dirty trick."

All these leading characteristics in British life, the
independence of spirit and the belief in voluntary effort,
the recognition of sound character as the basis of successful
action, and that respect for a certain code of conduct
which is shared by every stratum of society—all these you
will find reflected in the educational methods of the
country.   The character of the nation being what it is,
it was bound to reproduce these traits in its schools, and
once they had been bred in the schools they in turn
have helped to strengthen and preserve the same tendencies in the nation as a whole.   Thus it is typical that
the most original and the best-known British educational
experiment has been the so-called public schools, which
have owed less than any other department of our education to the State, and which have been entirely developed
by the initiative of individuals.   The public schools—
rather puzzlingly they are called public schools although,
in fact, they are privately owned and managed—are at
present the schools of only a small minority, the children
of those who can afford to pay fairly substantial fees for
them.   But that is altering fast, and it is already clear
that the war will put an end to what is left of that economic
privilege, and that the school of the future will be a sort
of combination of the public voluntary school and the
less expensive school controlled by a public authority.

But the public schools have been so widely imitated elsewhere, and have influenced our other schools so much, and are so much more distinctively British, or perhaps it would be more accurate to say so much more distinctively English, than any of our other schools, that it is fair to mention them first. Characteristically they were created, not by State action, not even by educational theorists, but by a handful of practical schoolmasters early in the last century. Characteristically, too, they were not invented; they were developed out of something different which was already in existence—out of the six or seven ancient schools—Eton, Rugby and others—which, for one reason or another, had ceased to serve the needs only of their own locality, and had formed the habit of taking boarders instead of day-boys. They were mostly very rough, undisciplined societies, in which a boy might learn to stand up for himself, to fight and to swear, but did not learn much else of value. Then, early in the nineteenth century, Dr. Arnold of Rugby decided that the object of education should be to turn out God-fearing citizens. And he created the monitorial system, the invention on which the British public school system may be said to be founded. That is to say, he handed over most of the discipline of the school to the boys, the elder boys, themselves.

Then take the ancient Universities of Oxford and Cambridge, which have also grown up without State control, and are therefore perhaps more characteristic than the younger Universities of London, Birmingham, and elsewhere. There, too, surely is something unlike anything else in the world. And again the difference is profoundly characteristic. For these are universities whose intellectual standards are as high as those of any university in the world, but which, like the public schools, have not been content with intellectual standards only. Everyone who has been to Oxford or Cambridge will tell you that at least as valuable as the education which comes from books and lectures, and even from the personal tutorial system—developed there as it has been developed nowhere else in the world—is the education to be got from eating, living, playing, and sitting up half the night to argue about everything in heaven and earth, with the men of every class and type whom you meet there.   Here, too, in the clusters of grey old palaces by Isis or Cam you have something which has grown unplanned through the centuries, from experiment to experiment, until it became as charming and as illogical as England herself.

At first sight the countless elementary and secondary schools, controlled partly by the State and partly by local public authorities, may seem less distinctively British because they are more like their counterparts in many other countries.   Yet here, too, you find the characteristic national tendencies at work.   For decades, for one thing, elementary education developed virtually without State assistance, through the efforts of private individuals and societies, mostly religious societies.   And when in 1870 the first long step was taken to the present universal compulsory free education, the schools soon developed another characteristically English compromise.   In many other countries today only one opinion on everything may be taught to school children.   But here we were so afraid that children might be taught the belief only of one Church or only one political party that an elaborate (and not very satisfactory) compromise was arrived at by which religious teaching became the lowest common denominator, so to speak, of all the various Churches, and to this day local authorities think it improper, when appointing a teacher, to inquire as to his religious or political opinions.   No doubt in some ways this is a pity, but at any rate most people will agree that it is better than allowing only one sort of person to teach and only one sort of view to be held. And anyone who examined the publicly controlled schools today would find that although the intellectual standard is constantly being raised, and as a matter of fact the teaching is often better in the local authority's secondary school than in the expensive so-called public school, here too much besides mere book teaching is going on. The health, the nutrition, the whole personality of the children is the constant care of the devoted men and women who labour in the schools. Almost every day as I go to or from my work, I meet the children of two different girls' schools, one controlled by a public authority, the other a more expensive private affair. It is the girls of the cheaper school who look healthier, livelier, and better dressed. The State may be in control, but it has never wished to crush out, and it certainly has not crushed out, the personal initiative of the teachers, thousands of whom you will find spending many hours each week, voluntarily and unpaid, out of school hours, to organise the games, or stimulate the hobbies, of the children. The result is that mass education has not produced a mass mind, as some feared it might. The Cornishman is still a Cornishman and the Scot still a Scot. And thanks to an educational system which reflects the stubborn individuality of our people, these islands are still full of varied opinions and varied personalities, but still capable of sinking differences and becoming in the hour of national peril a people of one will and one faith.

Martin Armstrong

THE VILLAGE PUB

THE VILLAGE PUB. What is a village pub? Why, says
somebody, everyone knows what a village pub is: it's the
place where the villagers go to drink beer. Wrong. Or
if it's not wrong, it's such a hopelessly inadequate definition that it's as good as wrong. It's like defining a railway
station as a place where you go to stick a label on a bag.
No, the village pub is something much more than a place
where you go to drink beer. You go there at the end of
the day's work, or for a brief interval in the middle of it,
to meet your friends, have a nice quiet sit-down or a game
of darts, and discuss everything from broad beans to
Hitler. Also, admittedly, you go there because you're
thirsty, very thirsty, after many hours of work.

But even that doesn't include all the functions of the
village pub—nowhere near. For the village pub is,
besides, the only means of communication with the village
as a whole, short of calling personally at every house.
You might think that, if you wanted to tell the village
something important, you could stick up a poster on the
village notice-board or have circulars distributed to every
house. Well, you can do that, but it won't do you much
good. The village won't read your poster; and as for
your circulars, in the present urgent need of waste paper
the village knows well enough what to do with *them*.
What you actually do, to put your information across, is
something much simpler than that. You simply drop a
remark about it at the pub, and instantly, as if you had
dropped a penny in the slot, the machine gets to work,
and without any fuss the desired result supervenes. At

least, that is how we do it at the White Horse, and the White Horse is, in its essentials, very much like the Golden Lion, the Black Bull, the Blue Bear, the Red Cat, the Little Green Man, and all the other hospitable animals that cover our English countryside.

So let me leave the subject of village pubs in general and set about defining the White Horse in particular. The best way I can do so is to give you a few concrete instances. I want some young cabbage plants for my vegetable garden. If I lived in a town, I suppose I would buy them at a shop or order them by post. *Here* I simply go to the White Horse and mention the fact. " Does anybody happen to know if anybody has any spare cabbage plants ? "

" Yes," says somebody, " Jim Soandso has some. I'll let him know you're wanting a few."

A day or so later I find a newspaper parcel on my doorstep. It contains three dozen cabbage plants. In course of time I meet Jim Soandso at the White Horse. " You found your plants ? " he asks. Now there's no need, when he asks you that question, to burst into a great froth of politeness: " Oh yes, yes. Thank you very much indeed. Very kind of you; very kind of you, I'm sure." No; none of that. All you say is: " Yes, thanks; I found them. Good strong plants, too."

After some conversation I ask Jim Soandso if he doesn't feel like joining me in another pint. Well, he replies, he wouldn't wonder if he did. I order the drinks, he wishes me good luck, and the transaction is complete. · Now, *there's* a nice human way of doing things.

Here's another example, something of a different kind. Some years ago our Parish Council, of which I happened to be chairman at the time, was ordered to discover and plot out on a large-scale map the exact course of all the footpaths and rights-of-way in the parish area. It was suggested by the authorities that the best way to get at the

facts was to question the oldest inhabitants. But oldest
inhabitants don't *like* to be questioned. They think it
probable—and in nine cases out of ten they're right—that
you're trying to find out more than it's good for you to
know. And so they're bored, noncommittal, evasive,
even misleading.

We knew this, sympathised with it, and so we used a
more tactful method. I and a fellow councillor simply
went to the White Horse for our customary drink and,
while drinking, got into an argument about the course of
a certain old footpath. " Do you know," said one of us,
fumbling in his pockets, " do you know, I believe I have
a map on me, if only I could find it." So he had. What
a bit of luck! He fished it out, spread it on the bar, and
the argument continued. The oldest inhabitants listened
in amused, then in scornful, silence. Presently one of them
could stand it no longer. " No, no; that's all wrong.
Path don't go that way; never did." He appeals to the
other oldest inhabitants, and soon it is we who are silent
and the oldest inhabitants who are arguing. They even
rise from their benches and approach the map. " Now,
show us where the church is." " Here it is. That black
cross is it." " Right. Well, the path skirts round by the
churchyard there, then cuts across . . . here you are . . .
across the corner of that there field . . ." and so on. In
half an hour we have learnt all that the oldest inhabitants
can teach us about footpaths and rights-of-way.

Now I'll give you quite a recent example, a war-time
example, of how we manage things here. The Parish
Council received, through the Rural District Council, a
communication from the Ministry of Supply, asking them
to organise the collection of scrap-iron. Our chairman
asked me to undertake the job. I did, and in due course I
received from the Ministry some beautiful posters. I went
round the village and I selected a place for a dump, an
ideal place. It was the village pound, where in old days

they used to shut up strayed animals—sheep, cows, and suchlike. Then I stuck up the posters, which asked the public, in lovely large letters, to bring all their scrap-iron to the dump. Of course I already knew all about posters and their effect, or lack of effect, on our village; but these were such beautiful posters and I was dazzled by them. I really did believe that, this time, posters would work. So I stuck them up and lay low for a week. Then I went round and inspected the dump.

At first I thought it was completely empty. But I was wrong. No; in one corner, among the nettles, I detected a piece, a small piece, about a couple of feet perhaps, of iron guttering. So the posters really had had some effect. But not enough, I felt. I had the feeling that if this war was to be won—by *us*, I mean—we should have to supplement the posters with more practical measures. Having realised that, I went at once to the White Horse and ordered a pint of bitter. What else could I do?

I arrived there, as it happened, at a lucky moment, because there, also having a drink, was one of our local farmers. Would he lend me a horse and cart? " A horse and cart? What for? " " Why, to collect scrap-iron. This Government scheme, you know." " Oh, *that*! " Yes, certainly I could have a horse and cart and a man to drive it. " Only give us a day or two to finish getting in the hay: then you can have it, any evening you like." " Next *Tuesday* evening? " " Very good. Next *Tuesday* evening."

The next thing to do was to inform the village; but, seeing where I *was* at the moment, that was easy. I simply dropped the remark that next Tuesday evening I and the landlord of the White Horse (who had kindly volunteered help) and a couple more would be round with a horse and cart, hoping to find everyone's scrap-iron put out on the roadside where we could pick it up.

Tuesday evening arrived and at six-thirty we set off

with a fine prancing horse and a large, flat dray on which
we rode down the street for all the world like some sort
of travelling show.   And what we found on the roadsides
all along the village . . . well, it beggars description.
Old bedsteads, old bicycles, old stoves, boilers, oil-drums,
pots, pans, pails, kettles, and heaven knows what else.
It was unbelievable that so much junk could come out
of so small a village.   We packed it carefully on to the
dray, and when we had got a load we made for the dump.
    It was when we got there that the fun began.   We had
packed the junk so beautifully on to the dray that it was
almost impossible to persuade it to come off.   You
dragged and hauled at a bedstead and when at last you
managed to get it unfixed, you found you had a couple
of bicycles and an oil-stove hanging on to it.   Yes, the
*un*loading was twice the job the loading had been.   Well,
it was a lesson.   On the next journey we were more careful, or, rather, less careful.   We didn't pack things quite
so tight.   To and fro we went, travelling on board when
the dray was empty, walking by its side when it was full,
and by the time we had finished, the village pound was
full to the top.   There was about three foot of foam,
so to speak, rising up above the walls.   We stood back
and admired it.   Then we went off to the White Horse.
Once more, you see, we had to call upon the White Horse
to perform yet another of its multifarious functions.   In
other words, we were just dying of thirst.
    Well, we are now, perhaps, in a better position to build
up our definition of the village pub.   It is, let us freely
admit it at the outset, a hospitable place where you can
get a pint of bitter or mild or the two mixed together if
you prefer it, and wine and spirits and soft drinks too, for
that matter, if you prefer *them*.   And if you happen to be
very young you go there to buy chocolate, gob-stoppers,
and other luxuries, and your childish voice can be heard
chirping out its requirements round the corner of the

partition that separates you from the more seasoned customers. But the White Horse is also, as we saw in the case of the cabbage plants, a Ministry of Agriculture in embryo. From the incident of the footpaths and rights-of-way we perceive that it is also a sort of blend of the Home Office and Record Office, and it is clear from what I have told you of the little business of the scrap-iron that it also includes under its jurisdiction such matters as Communications, Transport, and Supply. And besides all this, it is a place where village affairs are discussed, schemes mooted and launched, influential persons run to ground, buttonholed, and appropriately and usefully influenced. In other words, a House of Commons and House of Lords rolled into one. And the beauty of it *is* that, unlike the Government departments which are recognised as such, we have no forms to fill in, no reports to write, no statistics, committees, commissions, sessions. Nothing of all that. The whole business is run by good-will and human contact, and if any hitch *does* happen to arise, well, as likely as not a pint of bitter will put it right.

What, then, is the village pub ? Obviously *this* is what it is: it is the unit of organisation of the British Empire.

William Holt

SELLING A BOOK

I'VE HAD SOME ups and downs in my life. One of the worst patches of luck I ever struck was when, after being mixed up in some labour disputes arising out of the introduction of the more-looms-per-weaver system I found myself unemployed. I'd four young children at the time. I couldn't get work anywhere. I fell into debt, owed money to the doctor, tradesmen, and my rent fell into arrears.

One day a friend of mine stopped me in the street and fished a letter out of his pocket. It was one that he'd evidently carried about with him for a long time, because it was soiled, the edges were frayed, and the paper was beginning to come apart where it had been folded. He unfolded it carefully and I recognised my own hand-writing. Tapping it with his finger he said, " This is *literature*. If you've written any more letters like this they ought to be published." I looked at him sceptically and said, " Would you buy a book made up of such material ? Would you pay, say, as much as three and sixpence for it ? " " Yes," he said, " certainly I would." And digging his hand into his pocket he pulled out three and sixpence. " Here you are," he said, " here's the money for mine now—in advance." Well, that seemed genuine enough. I ought to have told him to wait until I had a book to offer, but I didn't. I took the three and sixpence, and on my way home I bought some food for my family.

" I'll have to produce a book," I said to my wife jokingly, " or I might be had up for obtaining money under false pretences." And I told her what had happened.

" Well, why not ? " she said. " There'd be no harm done in trying."

Out of curiosity I sounded a few people I knew. There certainly seemed to be possibilities. I found a few ready customers, and my friend called at my cottage the next day and brought me some more orders—and cash. My brother had a packet of my letters, and I'd written many letters to friends. If I could collect all these together, maybe there'd be enough to make a book. I've knocked about the world a bit and lived rather an adventurous life, and in some of these letters I'd described my experiences. But to send the letters to a publisher was out of the question. My friends might be interested, but I was quite sure that no publisher would look at them as a business proposition, and anyhow I'd have to do something quickly if it was going to be of any use to me financially.

I'd no idea how much it would cost to print and bind an edition of a book, so I asked a local printer. I took along with me as a sample, a book which I took out of my bookshelf. I remember it was *Tales of Unrest* by Joseph Conrad. I compared the printer's estimate with figures I obtained from other printers and bookbinders in the district, and found that the lowest quotation came from a Halifax firm who offered to print and bind a thousand copies of a book with 75,000 words and cloth boards for £93. So I worked it out if I could sell a thousand copies at three and sixpence each net, I'd make a gross profit of £82. This would clear me of debt. It was very tempting. Before going any further, I decided to make a real test of the market. I began to knock at people's doors and canvass the idea in the Pennine valley where I lived. It was like diving into cold water when I knocked at the first doors. But, as in swimming, once I'd got right in I began to enjoy it. I got more orders and promises than I'd expected, and I jotted these names and addresses down in a notebook, When I'd got something like a hundred names and addresses I went along to the printer and showed him the list and asked if he'd take my order and allow me credit. " I shan't be able to pay you until I've sold the biggest part of them," I said. I told him quite frankly what circumstances I was in, but I did my best to convince him that I'd move heaven and earth and wouldn't rest until I'd sold every copy door-to-door. " I'll be able to sell them better when I've got some copies with me," I said. " Yorkshire folk don't like buying a pig in a poke." He was a man of generous and sporting instincts. He decided to take the risk and give me my chance.

By this time I was feeling quite excited about the book. I chose a bright saxe-blue cloth for the boards and insisted on the lettering on the spine being of real gold leaf—this cost me an extra five pounds. " Anyhow, it won't tarnish like gilt," I said. The binding he specified was strongly stitched and taped.

Now what should I call the book ? It wasn't easy to choose a title for such a hotch-potch sort of book. I was leaning back in my chair thinking about it at home and looking up at the ceiling—and there was an old parasol hanging from a hook over my head. It was one I'd brought back from Japan. I bought it at Kobe during a rainstorm, and it kept me dry on my way back to the ship. It was made of oiled paper and split bamboo; it could be used either as an umbrella or a parasol. " That's what I'll call the book! " I said—" *Under a Japanese Parasol.*" After all, I'd edited the book under it where it hung there, from the ceiling.

The books were delivered to my cottage in a motor-lorry. My house seemed to be full of books—in parcels of six. I broke open a few parcels at a time and wrapped each book separately in orange-coloured tissue-paper which contrasted pleasantly with the blue and gold when the package was broken open—I had no dust-cover on the book—and I packed a supply of books into my rucksack. I was able to carry twenty-five of them at a time, and I trudged from house to house, delivering first the ones which had been ordered, and then hawked the others from door to door. In one street alone in Todmorden—Industrial Street—I sold seventy-nine copies. As the days went by it became easier to sell them as the people who had bought copies began to talk about them. In a few weeks I'd sold out and paid my debts. I went on a tram to Halifax and paid the printer his bill of £98 in hard cash emptied from my rucksack on to his office table. The money was mostly in half-crowns and shillings. It took him a long while to count it. It was a grand sight for both of us.

" I've an order here from a bookseller," he said, " what shall I do with it ? "   " What's your lowest price for another thousand ? " I said. Well, he worked it out. Now that the type was set up it would only cost me £49. So this would allow a margin for trade discount. " Print another thousand," I said.

When I sent copies to the *Leeds Mercury*, the *Yorkshire Post*, the *Manchester Guardian*, the *Daily Herald*, and the *News-Chronicle*, the reviews which appeared were very encouraging and orders began to come in from booksellers. The *Leeds Mercury* sent a reporter to Todmorden to interview me. I sent out a further batch of review copies, hired a saloon car and went to London to break into the wholesale market.

The first place I visited there was a big wholesale firm in Portugal Street. I'd a great difficulty in getting to see the chief buyer, and when he spoke to me I saw by his accent that he was Scots. His attitude at first was discouraging, to say the least, but after a few minutes he melted and ordered one hundred copies for his chief railway bookstalls. Then he reached for the telephone and spoke to the chairman of one of the largest wholesale book firms in the world. " I'm sending you a man who is selling books," he said. " I want you to meet him. I've given him an order, and I'm sure you will too "— and he did. His chairman friend received me very charmingly and ordered another hundred copies. The sales manager rang up the *Evening News*. Within a few minutes I was interviewed and photographed. A column and three-quarters about the story of my book, together with my photograph, appeared in that paper. It seemed that I was the first man in the world to do anything like this and make a success of it.

I sold out the rest of my second printing to the trade and returned north, where I negotiated better terms for a third printing of two thousand copies. At home I found a number of letters from London publishers inviting me to offer my next book to them, and my wife was very excited at my sudden good fortune. It had certainly come very fast. Actually only a few weeks had passed between poverty and desperation and what appeared to be success as an author. In fact, I'd suddenly become author, publisher, and bookseller all rolled into one.

And now let me tell you how this story of a book became a story of many books, and how I came to put books on wheels. My door-to-door bookselling had opened my eyes to the vast hinterland market for books. I saw no reason why books should not circulate like newspapers, in millions. It was just a matter—it seemed to me—of taking them to the door and making it easy for folk to buy them. So I designed on paper a small motor-body with roller shutters, waterproof, movable shelves, and electric lighting for rapid display at the road-side in any kind of weather. The machine was built for me by an engineering firm in Bradford. It was fitted with a 6-horse-power motor-cycle engine, and the firm supplied the machine to me for £95 on hire-purchase terms.

When the machine was delivered I loaded up with four hundred copies of *Under a Japanese Parasol*, and set off to London down the Great North Road. I traded my books this time in bookshops for copies of books by other authors, and in this way built up my first general stock. To save expense and time I slept in the body of the machine, among the books, for a few hours on the roadside near Stamford on my way down and back.

Now, I'd found in my door-to-door bookselling by rucksack that there were lots of people who were willing to buy books, but they couldn't put all the cash down at once. They offered to pay " so much a week." I remember one dear old lady, an old lame weaver who was living in a cottage all by herself. " I'll buy one of your books," she said, " but I can only pay you sixpence a week. I've heard about the book and I would like to read it. It's always out when I go to the library." " Yes, and I'd like you to read it, Sarah," I said. She handed me sixpence and I took a book out of my rucksack. " Here you are," I said. " You might as well be reading it while you're paying for it." " Oh no ! "—she was shocked at the idea—" I mustn't read it till I've paid for it. It wouldn't be honest." I couldn't persuade her to have it until she'd paid the full amount in sixpences. One day, a few months later I felt a tug at my sleeve in the street. It was old Sarah the weaver. " I've been trying to catch you for a while now, but you walk so fast. I've read your book," she said, " and I have enjoyed it; look ! " —she was trying to put something into my hand. " Here's sixpence," she said, " towards your next book. You must have been put to big expense."

Well, authors who publish in the orthodox way don't enjoy the privilege of meeting readers like Sarah! I remember a farmer, too, who bought one of my books on the condition that if he didn't like it I'd have to have it back. I met him after he'd read it. " Well, what do you think about it ? " I said. " It's very fair," he said. " Well, have I to take it back ? " " No," he said, " I think I'll keep it."

Well, to cut a long story short, fired with the idea of a big fleet of motor-bookshops and libraries touring Great Britain I went up to Manchester to raise capital with a view to forming my first company. I got into touch with a stockbroker, a chartered accountant, and several business-men, and succeeded in raising £2,000. We floated a private limited company in Manchester. After a year of successful experiment we increased our nominal capital to £15,000 and issued 9,000 fully-paid pound shares. Our fleet of motor libraries spread out over the country as far as Blackpool, Birmingham, London, and Brighton. Later on I founded a second company and launched another fleet of vehicles based on the West Riding of Yorkshire.

So you might call this a story of a book that became many books, of how I started by carrying books on my back, and then put them on wheels.

Group-Captain M. G. Christie, C.M.G., D.S.O., M.C.

NIGHT FLYING

LITTLE OR NO flying in darkness or even semi-darkness was attempted before 1914 ; 'planes were felt to be too unstable, engines far too unreliable. Indeed, those of us who flew prior to the Great War found enough adventure in flying by day. We hadn't much surplus power to play with: two-seater Service aircraft only carried a 70 horse-power engine, developing a maximum speed of about 60 miles per hour. The best-designed aeroplane in 1914 could not lift more than one-third of the load which a similar sized 'plane of 1940 construction can carry.

After the outbreak of the Great War, however, the problem of defending our towns and industrial districts against night attacks from enemy airships had to be tackled quickly. You see, the Zeppelins had one great advantage over aeroplanes—even if all its engines failed simultaneously, a Zeppelin could still remain in the air while the crew overhauled the defective mechanism. In 1914, the number of our anti-aircraft guns was very limited, so that already in the autumn of that year we had to send up aeroplanes on night patrol, carrying one or two small bombs, when the approach of a Zeppelin was reported. Our pilots had to try to climb above the airship and drop these twenty-pounder bombs on to its enormous hull: one such bomb could easily wreck it and set the hydrogen gas on fire.

I think airmen from our R.N.A.S. were the first to tackle this tough job; they faced all the difficulties of trying to locate enemy airships with the uncertain aid of very few ground searchlights; they ran the risk of having to make a forced landing in the dark, either through engine failure or through inability to find an aerodrome to land on. Remember, not twenty serviceable aerodromes existed in all England in August 1914—and those were neither equipped for night operations nor marked by beacon lights.

The aerodrome lighting system was extremely primitive; no floodlights to enable the pilot to see the ground ahead of him when taking off and landing; no illuminated signs marking taller obstacles on the outer edge of the aerodrome, such as high chimneys, buildings, trees, etc., with which the 'plane might collide. Only a small fairway across the aerodrome heading into wind, roughly 400 yards in length and 50 in width, was marked with paraffin flares, i.e. paraffin and cotton waste burning in open tins or buckets; these flares spaced 50 yards apart were laid out in the shape of a capital " L." This denoted also that the wind was blowing from the short arm of the " L " exactly parallel to the long arm. Supposing we are starting out on a night patrol on a cloudy, moonless night, under conditions such as prevailed in 1914. Well, first we taxi out to No. 1 flare, then put on full engine and race up the flare path, keeping parallel to the flares marking the long arm of the " L." By this method we steer dead into wind and prevent our machine from yawing off its all-clear course; gradually we coax the aeroplane off the ground into the darkness ahead. We mustn't let our machine get out of control while climbing the first 500 feet, for if we make a mistake there will be insufficient height to recover equilibrium, and we are bound to smash. So we must strain our eyes to spot the distant horizon, for then we can check up whether we are flying on a level keel and climbing at the right angle or not ; the only means we have of reading the dials of the instruments which show our flying speed, compass course, oil pressure, engine revolutions, etc., is a small hand-torch. It is a tricky job to fly on a really dark night without constantly referring to the instrument-board. I remember once myself, while returning from a Zeppelin hunt I suddenly ran into a murky fog at roughly 1,000 feet altitude. Being unprepared I was quickly in trouble and lost all sense of balance; the wires on the machine began to sing, the wind seemed to blow from all directions into the cockpit. I shut off the engine, and a second later realised that the aeroplane was flying almost upside down immediately over a row of high poplar trees. I just managed to right her in time, and then flew around, hedgehopping, until with great relief I sighted the flares of my aerodrome.

But now let's get back to our own night flight and assume that we've climbed above the clouds and can no longer see the ground. Our maps are useless; the compass is misleading since we do not know the real strength and direction of the wind at this level.

Usually the wind strength grows and its direction alters considerably as altitude increases; thus we may easily drift many miles off our course. Here's an example. Early in 1915 a young R.F.C. pilot was ordered to deliver a machine to a squadron in France from some-where in the South of England. He flew east by compass over dense clouds for a time and then came down through them to determine his whereabouts. Seeing a large stretch of water below him he continued his flight till the coast hove in sight. Shortly afterwards he landed in a field to get his bearings and began to address a farm labourer in his best school French. He drew blank. His English was more successful; he had landed in Essex after flying not across the Straits of Dover as he thought but across the Thames Estuary. A strong wind had carried him almost due north.

Well, to continue with our imaginary night flight—if we want to keep a check on our course, we must keep below the clouds. Certain things show up clearly, such as the coastline marked by the phosphorescent surf, white chalk quarries, the dim light reflected by rivers, lakes, reservoirs, the burnished metal surfaces of railway lines.

By the way, one of the most unpleasant dangers to pilots on night patrol is ground fog, which can form very quickly and is very deceptive because from above it looks like a cloud layer; we cannot recognise from an altitude of several thousand feet whether the clouds below us extend down to the ground or not. Nowadays pilots can be warned by radio from the ground about weather conditions, but in 1914 our aeroplanes carried no wireless sets of any kind. And now we must end our night flight by landing on our aerodrome. Not so easy with only the flickering light of a few small paraffin flares. We must throttle our engine and adjust our gliding angle, so that our aeroplane will be within a few feet of the ground when reaching No. 1 flare. We then slowly flatten out and let the machine more or less land itself.

During 1915 Zeppelin activities by night over England increased greatly, whilst in France single German 'planes raided near targets occasionally. One night in July 1915 a German 'plane dropped seven light bombs on the town of St. Omer nearly sixteen miles behind our lines. I happened to be on duty at the aerodrome, so calling my gunner quickly, I got ready to take off. There was one chance in a million of intercepting the German, for as soon as my engine started, I could no longer hear the enemy machine—and there were practically no searchlights around. However, we sped off in the dark and left the ground. It was a bit uncanny, but the horizon soon came into view, and night-flying turned out easier than I had anticipated. We climbed gradually to 7,000; there was no sign of our enemy. After flying around for an hour, I decided that we'd done all we could. Unable to determine our whereabouts, I steered a westerly course by compass for half an hour to make sure we were on our own side of the lines, and then glided down cautiously towards what dimly appeared to be open flat fields. The earth came up close, so I cut out the engine. The machine made contact with the ground at a speed of perhaps 45 miles per hour, swiped off its undercarriage and squatted down like a broody hen. We were unhurt. We had had great good luck, because we happened fortunately to have come down in very open country in a bean-field.

I returned to England in the spring of 1916, and found great progress. Several specially trained anti-Zeppelin squadrons were stationed around greater London, and I was lucky enough to be put in charge of one. The whole area was packed with searchlights and a network of guns and listening-posts extended south and east to the sea coast. Up to that time one or two Zeppelins had been damaged by gunfire but only one destroyed over England. Several engagements between our aeroplanes and enemy airships had taken place with no visible results.

Unfortunately our 'planes could not climb so fast as the Zepps. Again, *twelve* thousand feet was our absolute *maximum* altitude, whereas some enemy airships could touch 18,000 feet after unloading their bombs. Further, when on patrol at 10,000 feet we could barely do 60 miles per hour, very little faster than a Zepp; thus if the searchlights showed up the enemy we could hardly catch him unless he was near and not above us. Our 'planes were now equipped with Lewis guns firing incendiary tracer bullets. We had many arguments as to the best method of attack, most pilots thought that by flying two or three hundred feet beneath the Zepp and shooting upwards so as to puncture the hull in very many different places, the incendiary bullets must start a fire somewhere. But this spraying method failed in actual practice. The problem finally solved itself. One misty night in the late summer of 1916, Lieutenant Robinson, already a veteran at night-flying, was on patrol at about 10,000 feet on the outskirts of North London ; suddenly an enemy airship appeared in a searchlight beam no great distance away. He went all out to catch the hesitating enemy. Just as he was getting close up behind the airship she put on speed and climb and began to pull away from him. In desperation Robinson fired a long burst into the fleeing target, aiming at one spot on the tail-end of the huge hull. His concentrated fire tore a big hole in the gasbag, his tracers ignited the escaping hydrogen as it mixed with the air. The trick was done. The doomed airship staggered around and fell to earth like a flaming torch, and Robinson, who was then below and gliding down to his own aerodrome, had difficulty in dodging the burning wreckage. Thus the right tactics revealed themselves. Several more Zeppelins fell victims to our aeroplanes that year, and our night-fliers soon became very proficient.

Nesbitt Sellers

ENVIRONMENT

THE FIRST AND most obvious change in anyone after he
has joined the services is, of course, his physical condition.
Physical training, drill, a different diet, absolutely regular
meals, sleeping and waking hours (regulated to the last
minute in some cases)—all these make up his new environment.   And naturally in 99 cases out of 100 there must be
a fairly marked physical change.

All this is, after all, a matter of common experience.
But there is, I think, another change, and a far more
important one for the individual too.   The fact that it is
less obvious to others probably makes it less obvious to
him.   What is this change ?   Well, may I call it a mental
change ?   The change in one's general outlook caused by
a fundamentally new environment.

It's a strangely subtle and elusive affair.   My experience
is that it is quite gradual.   Indeed, it is impossible to be
sure of all its manifestations.   Suddenly from time to time
one pops up and hits you in the face with a resounding
smack.   At first you blink your eyes and shake your head,
and then you see in a flash that you have changed.   Once
realised, you fall to wondering what other changes have
been wrought in you by your new environment.   And
you watch for others.

When I joined the Royal Air Force last September to
be trained as a pilot, the life was so vigorous and unusual
that I used all my energies keeping my head above water.
The first three or four months were more or less a mental
black-out, except for study and routine thinking.   One
didn't want to listen to the wireless, to read books or

newspapers, and one seldom indulged in serious conversation. It was enough to concentrate on getting the feeling of a new occupation.

Then came the first leave. I went back, full of life, to London. It was a blow to find one's friends did not seem to be as much a part of you as before. Try as you might, you could not get back into the swing of the old life. The design seemed to have gone. So I was actually glad to get back to my training school.

I know now that this was an " in-between " period. I have again been on leave in London. All was perfect. I was not out of touch. I had not lost contacts.

The really astounding point is the simple and entirely unexpected way all this turmoil, these effects of a new environment, were revealed. I was sitting in my dentist's surgery as I had dozens of times before. Out of the windows I could see the traffic swirling round Russell Square from Southampton Row. But this day I caught myself. I found I was not looking at the traffic at all. I was looking up at a little patch of blue sky wedged between two tall buildings and blocked out occasionally by passing clouds. And I was thinking: " It would be a good day for flying, once above those clouds."

I caught myself thinking this, and I said to my dentist, " Good Lord, what's happened? Do you know what I was thinking then? " And told him.

That was what first set me on the track of this " Mental-change idea." Let me give you some other simple examples. I gave up smoking when war began. When I came to the flying training school, where I am now stationed, I started pipe-smoking again. I smoke an ounce a day—but when I am in London I don't smoke at all. I've often wondered why this was. I suppose it's because I've got such a lot to do when I'm on leave in London.

A few days ago I was dreaming in a train going through

the Midlands. I saw a windmill. My spontaneous reaction was, "Damn, it's stationary. What a pity it's not working. Now I can't tell which way the wind is blowing." This, of course, was the new complex of flying showing itself.

I went for a cross-country run with two friends over fields near our aerodrome. It was a new land, utterly different from the land we saw from the air—yet it was the same. We saw hills and ridges we had never noticed before. We found ourselves looking at fields intently as we ran through them. Why?—to see if they were large enough, smooth enough to make forced landings in. Such is the effect of environment. A few years ago in New Zealand I looked in fields to see if there were rabbits to shoot. A few months ago I looked in fields in England to see if the land had been ploughed up to grow more food. Now I look for landing surfaces.

I was a journalist in Fleet Street on a great newspaper, living a free, vastly interesting and amusing life. Now I am one of a hundred or so living in a drill-hall at a flying training school. Perhaps I am now an airman who is a journalist—perhaps, I hope, I am a journalist who is an airman. I don't know. We are a mixed bag—18 to 30 years old; clerks, a racing motorist, yachtsmen, a railroad engineer, students, a social worker, insurance men. Those who are 18 act as though they are 22 and those who are 25 often seem to be 18. We have lost the sense of time. The unemployed used to do that. One does the same thing at sea ; there you don't care about times or days or dates. Neither do we—much.

In our drill-hall where we sleep and spend much of our time, we have a great and strident wireless. There is always noise. Yet there was always noise in Fleet Street. I worked to the sound of typewriters tapping, people talking, and telephones ringing. But now I find— many of us find—we would often sell our souls for silence.

So we go out into the silence of the countryside—not just for a change of scene, but for silence. Often a young Londoner and I go out—we hear a bird singing in the twilight; we listen to a stream rippling over boulders. Sometimes we part and go our separate ways in solitude.

That morning we may have been roaring over those very fields in our noisy monoplanes, disturbing every living thing for miles around and liking it. Can it be that our environment sends us to extremes?

I rather think so. Our wireless may be blaring out a gay and popular tune. The drill-hall is alive with action and noise, someone twiddles the dial. Beethoven, Liszt, or Wagner is among us. In a few moments the drill-hall is quiet. People sit down on their beds, or walk over to the wireless and stand hands in pockets, heads down, looking at the set.

We are a strange crowd. As part of the crowd—remember I was a journalist and therefore never wholly free from the observer's attitude of separateness—I have reached dizzier heights and plumbed darker depths in the shortest spaces of time. I notice the same in others. Quick and intensified reactions to small things—a chance remark; a thoughtless smile. Then chaos.

We seem to be striving after, seeking, permanent things.

Talking among ourselves, we find there is often a general feeling of boredom. In one expression of our lives we are conscious and violent pleasure seekers, but as such we do not really achieve much real satisfaction. Pleasure seeking, too, becomes boring, especially when its practice is strictly confined and limited. So there is this quest for, to use a cliché, " things that matter."

In civil life such ideas rarely entered my head, or if they did, not as a plan to be followed. Yet now it is a part of the pattern of things. I notice chaps read more books these days ; a miscellaneous collection, but not trash—Norman Douglas, Freud, Linklater, Cronin, Shakespeare,

H

Maurois.   And there is the ritual of solving innumerable crossword puzzles.   The thrill of good conversation is now very real.   All this has grown up gradually in this new environment, and with it a return to reading newspapers. Incidentally, how much more appreciated is the photograph of, say, snowdrops in a wood than, perhaps, a tank being inspected by some general.

One of the most beneficial changes produced by this new environment is that it teaches in no uncertain manner the value of personal liberty.   All who, to put it shortly, live for democracy have a sense of personal liberty.   Sometimes its value is not appreciated—it is just taken for granted.   Not so with us now.   Hand in hand with personal liberty goes individuality.

In the services we must all conform more or less to a general scheme which permits no exceptions.   In the R.A.F., in particular, men are selected for their personal qualities.   They can scarcely be expected to become cogs in a machine.   As far as I can see, this is not desired. Clearly it is not desirable.   But it is unavoidable to some degree.   Is it not, in a way, a good thing that by devices and tricks, however small or trivial, men add a little frill or a little twist of their own to what would otherwise be merely a mass, herd-like reaction ?

I've been told that it is not unusual for men to say that even when the war is won they would rather stay in the Forces.   Well, I haven't noticed that so far among my companions.   This is probably because they are the type who would not have allowed themselves to sink into a rut in civil life.   So they find no escape—they have no need to.   But very often they find help in escaping back, as it were, now into their past lives.

I have not indulged in a string of sugar platitudes about how happy we are in our work.   I've assumed that you know we wouldn't be trying to be pilots if we didn't want to.   Bearing that in mind—as we always do—let's look ahead. That is the last of these effects of environment that I want to mention.

In civil life one chattered a bit about the world after the war. One hoped but did not feel sure that there would be a chance of taking an active part in building a really new world. But now we are certain—as certain as the day is day—that we are going to play a big part— a mighty big part—in the new order. It is going to be our new world, and we are going to see that we make it.

EDITOR'S NOTE

I first met Nesbitt Sellers about three years ago. He was then on the staff of *The Times*, and came not infrequently to Broadcasting House. His tall, thin figure and cavernous voice gave him on first acquaintance a slightly melancholy air. He was in truth the very opposite—a gay, cheerful, humour-loving soul; generous to a fault, friendly, and highly intelligent. He had an acute power of observation and a ready pen, which stood him in good stead as a reporter. Later he joined the R.A.F. and, on one of his visits to London, was talking in his usual animated manner, this time about the difference between his life as a civilian and his life as an airman. We discussed the effect of environment, and I suggested, with his own experience to draw on, that he should broadcast a Talk on this subject. " Environment " duly arrived and was duly broadcast.

I last saw him in November, when I lunched with him. A week or two later he was killed in a flying accident. Hector Bolitho has sent me the following appreciation:

" I think that Nesbitt had less meanness in him— meanness of mind and spirit—than anybody I have ever known. It was a privilege to have his friendship, because of the rigid principles which guided his own life and the lenience with which he judged others. His sense of humour was a joy to me—nobody else's letters were more welcome. But they were never a worthy substitute for the actual pleasure of being with him and hearing that deep stomach laugh which simply made everybody near him feel ten years younger. What a terrible loss of talent—and character! He wrote well, he spoke well, and he was a noble-hearted friend."

Sir Adrian Boult

A VILLAGE CHORAL FESTIVAL

NINE A.M. ON a rather chilly spring morning. A crowd of singers packed into a small waiting-room, and in the distance tentative sounds of the first victims struggling to sing their sight test. All around us is intense excitement. " What will this year's judge be like ? " " Is the sight test hard ? Anyhow, the people who are singing now are making it sound pretty frightful." " Did you get all your milking done before you started ? " " I did all but three, but, then, my Johnny is twelve now and can really manage quite well when I'm gone." " I just got all my baking done, but they had to keep the 'bus waiting three minutes for me."

You see, the Petersfield Festival Choir is made up of country folk from remote districts, and for many it is a real struggle to get the essential part of their day's work done before eight, or even seven-thirty when some oɪ the 'buses start. But the Festival is the event of the year for many of them, and I think even those who live within easy reach of the cinemas of Petersfield, and those for whom an evening in Portsmouth is not too rare a luxury, still find the Festival a different kind of thrill: making their own active contribution to the performance of great music instead of just sitting back and listening.

But I should really have begun with a description oɪ the framework of the Festival. Let us remember that this is just an example of a type which flourishes all over the country. The very first was started at Kendal on the edge of the Lake District fifty-five years ago by Miss Mary Wakefield, whose family still help to run it. And places like Dorking, Newbury, Chelmsford, Winchester, Truro, Newtown, Andover, and many others have flourishing Festivals which are based on the principle of the pooling of a number of separate village choirs to sing fine music together.

These choirs usually spend the whole winter practising. They may give separate concerts, but their final object is to come together on the Festival Day and join into one large chorus to rehearse and perform the music they have been studying all through the winter.

Now let us trace the Festival Year from its beginning, late in the summer, to the great day which is usually fixed just before or just after Easter. Its beginning is the sitting of the Music Committee, consisting usually of local musicians with one or two professionals to help. They draw up the programme scheme for the winter's work— I put it in this way because they have to remember that it isn't just the single occasion for which they are pre- paring—but they are carrying the responsibility for choosing music that will stand the hard test of being studied note by note, part by part, once a week or oftener through the long winter. These choirs work hard, their conductors, who may be the village parson or the schoolmistress or anyone else, put them through it to such good purpose that many choirs know every note and every word by heart, and so are able to give the conductor a response that would do credit to the foremost choral societies in the land.

The syllabus is printed and circulated somewhere about October, and during November there is a meeting at which the Festival conductor joins the choir con- ductors, accompanists, and sometimes a picked quartet from each choir, who can sing through the whole pro- gramme and get the general hang of how the music ought to go. At Petersfield, where I have conducted for nearly twenty years, they know a good deal about my

way of tackling all the problems, but, even so, time is
sometimes allowed for a talk on voice-training and interpretation, or some of the other principles behind conducting.   This meeting usually takes place a few weeks after
most of the choirs have begun their winter's work, and
so the conductors have already met some of their problems
and difficulties, and these can be discussed.   I always
enjoy this preliminary day very much, for I find I learn
a great deal by hearing about other people's problems.

Four or five months now elapse, during which the choirs
work on at their music.   I should explain that the Petersfield choirs vary considerably in their achievement, and
in peace-time the Festival has, besides the Children's Day,
three separate grown-up days at which the music set
varies in difficulty and length, and choirs win or lose
their way from one division to another on a rather loosely
good-natured league principle.   Many of them vary their
Festival work with other things: a Carol Concert at
Christmas-time or perhaps a performance of part of
The Messiah.   Then there is usually a concert a few
weeks before the Festival, when they sing their Festival
music to a local audience whose contributions help to
pay for the choir's food and transport on the Festival
Day.

I have had some interesting notes on the general
influence of the village choral society from clergymen
and other specialists in welfare.   One parson told me
that when his choir started its rehearsals in the autumn
all mischief making in the village came to a sudden end.
A surprisingly large percentage of the adult population
of a village will often be found in the choir, tiny hamlets
sending in choirs of twenty-five or more.

About a month before the Festival, choirs are collected
together in convenient places, usually but not always the
centre of the area, and a pretty thorough combined
rehearsal is held, at which the whole programme is

covered by practically everyone who is to take part in it. It isn't possible at this stage to get perfection in every detail, but one can often make suggestions on points which can be further studied in the weeks that are left, and it is good to watch the conductors, scattered about amongst their choirs, marking their copies industriously as any hint is dropped which opens up a new line of thought.

Now we come to the Festival Day. I have tried to sketch the atmosphere of the opening competition: sight reading, always the most dreaded part of the day, which is good to get finished at once. After the choirs have got through this ordeal, they may stay inside the hall and hear the judge's comments.

The organisation of these competitions varies enormously from festival to festival. For my part, I am satisfied that the best festivals are those at which all competitions are finished early in the day, and the rest of the time is devoted to rehearsing for the evening performance. I like to see every choir enter for every competition, and I think every bar of the final festival programme should form part of the competition schedule. Many festivals are unable to simplify things to this extent; they feel bound to vary their scheme with competing quartets, ensembles of various kinds, and even solo competitions.

My feeling about it is this: the object of a festival is surely to give the longest opportunity, to as many people as possible, of soaking in great music, and of having that experience directed by competent musicians. Let me take one extreme. A young lady enters for a solo competition. She has one or two songs or pieces to learn. She learns them well, and we hope gets competent advice (which she probably has to pay for) while learning them. She then plays them at the competition, and her efforts are criticised by the judge in thirty seconds perhaps or a couple of minutes at most. That is the end of it; sometimes if she wins the prize she plays or sings the same pieces once more at a public concert later in the day. Now for the other extreme: your village choir member spends an hour or two every week through the winter sitting with friends old and new, and it is no uncommon sight to see the squire's son sitting next to his father's ploughboy; they work together on fine, big music under the guidance of a keen amateur whose competence is at any rate adequate; they may have the added fun of singing in several village concerts during the winter, and perhaps even two or more villages may join together for some special church or secular performance. And then on the Festival Day they hear their performance criticised by a judge who has far more time to devote to each entry, and I have recollections of wonderfully eloquent addresses by some of our greatest musicians summing up the detailed criticisms they have given. After that there are still several hours of work ahead with an experienced conductor, and the final thrill of singing it all again to a big audience, often with orchestral accompaniment and fine soloists. Surely this is a far fuller musical experience than learning a couple of solos and playing them through to a judge?

To go back now to the morning competitions. There may be several of these: first the sight test, then a madrigal or other unaccompanied work in which the individuality and musicianship of the conductor can be fully tested; then the test piece chosen by the judge from the main " work " of the day. This may be an oratorio, a cantata, or a big work like Verdi's and Brahms's Requiems, The Dream of Gerontius, or even Bach's B Minor Mass or the Matthew Passion complete without cuts. The morning usually finishes with competitions for works for separate men and women's voices, and a well-earned lunch comes next. Possibly here a short meeting between the judge and choir conductors can be arranged, at which the judge can amplify his criticisms and answer questions and appeals for constructive help which can be most valuable.

Competitions are undeniably useful: they help us " to pace each other on the road to excellence," as Sir Walford Davies has happily expressed it, but the ideal festival restricts its awards to challenge banners, pictures, and cups, which can be held for a year and can have the name of the winning village inscribed on it somewhere each time.

At the best-managed festivals the competitive part of the affair is absolutely forgotten from lunch onwards, and the individual singers—for instance, the two and a half tenors which one conductor once said she had—now find themselves part of a choir of two hundred enthusiasts, everyone of them knowing his music through and through. It isn't easy to realise this feeling if you haven't actually experienced it. The member of a choir of twenty or thirty is always conscious of a struggle to keep his part going against the other parts, particularly the all-powerful sopranos who often overweigh everyone else. Now he suddenly finds that he is surrounded by people who are all singing the same part as himself, and their enthusiasm and his can be concentrated into a fine volume of sound.

When I am conducting I try to arrange two separate rehearsals with a half-hour interval in between. These take a different character. At two o'clock we do a thorough analysis; we stop often to discuss principles and occasionally to throw a constructive remark to the conductors, whose notebooks and pencils are still at hand. We may even leave out easy passages if the work is long and the choirs competent. Then a short tea interval, and at five or so we begin a much more complete run-through of the whole programme. By this time we have been joined by the soloists; we have now got over the surprises caused by hearing a fine orchestra replacing the often

inadequate piano which has been our companion hither-
to, and our conductor leaves us alone much more, in fact
he rarely stops us now unless we have made some careless
mistake.   At the close of each piece or each movement, he
sometimes refers us back to points we have missed or
things we had done better at the early rehearsal; which
have to go better still at the performance.

Once more, dispersal and a meal.   A hurried change,
too, for orchestra and soloists, but evening dress is never
seen in the choir.   The concert should be (and usually
is) the brilliant culmination of this accumulated rehearsal
effort.   Rightly directed and rightly conserved at
rehearsal, this amateur material is capable of astounding
results, and if the programme is well balanced and contrasted, one finds that a concerto performance by a world-
famous artist falls naturally into the scheme, and by no
means sticks out above the general level.   I have seen
hardened critics deeply moved and exacting foreigners
amazed at the technical completeness, but far more at the
supreme power of interpretation which comes from those
who have naturally come to love great music through
taking a regular part in its performance themselves.
In my own experience of these last twenty years a remarkable development has taken place.   In the old days the
yearly festival performance was the only chance many of
the singers would have of hearing any music at all.   The
coming of wireless has changed all that, and I am often
impressed by the shrewdness of criticism of some of my
choir friends when discussing some of the broadcast
programmes they have been hearing.   This hearing will
have been far more complete because of their festival
experience; and I venture to claim that of the many
wonderful qualities shown by the British race, whether in
peace or war, its innate musicality, as seen at these festivals, is entitled to a prominent place.

L. A. G. *Strong*

"THE CALL"

WE DO THINGS in our own way in Puddle Parva, but we get
them done. Anyone who judged the probable result by
the preliminaries would make a grave mistake. Still, the
preliminaries, it must be admitted, are often a little odd.

A few months ago the powers that be gave instructions
as to what was to be done if our nearest town—let's call
it X—were bombed. It was assumed, cynically we
thought, that the inhabitants of X would disregard all
official instructions and do everything that they were
asked not to do. They would " stream " out of the town
into the surrounding country, and " stream " back again,
only to discover that they had suffered what was termed
" dehousement ": whereupon they would once more
" stream " out. A number of ladies in our village were
asked to act as recipients for this final stream, and distri-
bute it among an even larger number who should shelter,
for thirty-six hours, its component parts. (What magic
resided in the figure thirty-six, no one could determine;
but there it was.)

The volunteers were given their duties, and bidden be
ready at any time for a call to action. The call came the
other evening. It was delivered by a portly villager,
named Spriddle, whose love of drama had led him to
claim the rôle of messenger.

His first formula, " I brings yer a summons," was mis-
understood and resented by the ladies to whom it was
delivered; so that, by the time he reached us, he had
softened it down to, " You're wanted at the schoolroom,
urgent. The call 'as come."

L. A. G. STRONG

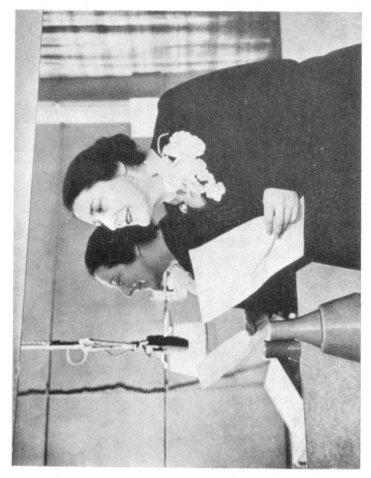

CLEMENCE DANE

I transmitted this message to Honoria, who was up-
stairs washing stockings. She swore, and sped off, clutch-
ing her list of instructions. What followed must be told
on her report: I was not privileged to be there. Still, I'm
sure we can trust her.

Arrived breathless at the schoolroom, she found four
out of a total strength of eleven ladies, and the second man
on the committee—the schoolmaster. The vicar's wife
sat restively in the chair, and discouraged all attempts at
conversation until such time as the missing members
should be found. Two more trickled in, wearing ag-
grieved expressions, and then Mr. Spriddle, wheezing
triumphantly, brought in two more. The vicar's wife
looked at them with nervous reproof, and asked Mr.
Spriddle if any others were coming along.

" Mrs. 'Unt should be here," he said. " I couldn't
locate 'er, not precise: but I lef' word, urgent."

" Then I think we might begin. That is, if we are a—
what d'you call it, Mr. Trafford ? "

" A quorum," said the schoolmaster. " Yes, Mrs.
Kingsley. Six is a quorum."

" Very well, then. We'll begin. What do we do
first ? "

" The minutes of the last meeting should be read."

" Oh dear."

" You'll find them in front of you, on the table."

Mrs. Kingsley eyed the book with distaste.

" Well, I suppose——"

" One moment, ladies." Mr. Spriddle had regained
his breath. " One moment, if you please. I 'ave to
tender an apology on be'alf of Mrs. Jones, 'oo is not
'ere, due to 'er bein' away."

" Go on," said a voice in the doorway. " Not really ? "

All heads turned, as a shapely figure, in green corduroy
slacks and yellow jumper, came into the room. Mrs.
Hunt was not regarded with unqualified approval in the

village. She was lavishly made up, she wore brilliant colours, spoke her mind, and, worst of all, she appeared as indifferent to what her neighbours did as she was to what they thought.

" 'Oo is not 'ere, due to 'er bein' away on 'oliday," pursued Mr. Spriddle. " Otherwise nothing would 'ave stopped 'er answerin' the call."

" Hear hear," said Mrs. Hunt, settling herself comfortably. " May we smoke ? "

The vicar's wife looked helplessly at the schoolmaster. " There's nothing against it," he said.

" I should hope not," said Mrs. Hunt. " Sorry if I'm late. I was in my bath. Beastly inconvenient time you chose, Spriddle."

" Ill-convenience," replied Mr. Spriddle, " is neither 'ere nor there. Which the choice was not mine, neither. When the call come, I was layin' flowers on my wife's grave. Did I 'esitate ? No. I lays the flowers on the ground, just as they was, and runs to answer the call. I shall go back and adjust them proper afterwards."

" No you won't. It'll be dark."

" In w'ich case, I shall do 'em first thing in the morning. Individual convenience don't signify w'en——"

The schoolmaster interrupted: " Might we get on with the business, do you think, Mrs. Kingsley ? "

" Very well. I suppose I'd *better* read the minutes. The last meeting of the Puddle Parva X Dehousement Reception Committee——"

" Order, order," said Mr. Spriddle to the meeting at large.

" ——was held on Thursday, September the 4th, at half-past four o'clock."

" In the afternoon."

" *Do* be quiet, Mr. Spriddle, please. We shall never get on, if you keep on interrupting."

Mr. Spriddle's face turned slowly purple. Before he

could protest, Mrs. Kingsley read on for some half minute in a rapid gabble, then stopped.

" Must I read this bit ? " she asked.

" What bit ? " asked the schoolmaster.

" This next bit."

" What is it about ? "

" About the raids they're supposed to have had in X."

" We know all that," said Mrs. Hunt. " Can't we get on to what matters ? "

" We know all of it, come to that," said another lady heavily.

" I think," suggested the schoolmaster, " that we ought to check over the different duties that were assigned, and see that each of us knows what we are expected to do."

" Sound man," approved Mrs. Hunt heartily. " Good idea."

The vicar's wife fussed at the pages.

" What page is it on ? " she inquired peevishly.

The schoolmaster got up.

" The pages aren't numbered," he said. " Shall I find the place for you ? "

" Oh ! Here it is ! The following specific duties were allocated and agreed. Secretarial work, Mr. Trafford."

The schoolmaster nodded.

" Interrogation and classification, Mrs. Hunt and Miss Jervis."

" I didn't quite realise," said Miss Jervis, "when I volunteered, the sort of questions I should be expected to ask. They are so—er—so very personal."

" W'en the call comes," said Mr. Spriddle, " we 'as to answer. All considerations of person and ill-convenience 'as to be put aside. Meself—I was busy——"

" Yes, yes, Mr. Spriddle. We know. You were laying flowers on your wife's grave. Yes. Let me see, where was I ? Oh yes. Cooking, Mrs. Brent. Why, Mrs. Brent—isn't that right ? "

" It is not right. I said I'd do anything *except* cook.
Don't you remember ? "

" Oh, well. There must have been a mistake. Let me
see, now—who *did* say she would cook ? Was it you,
Mrs. Hunt ? "

" It was not. You read me out a minute ago. Interrogation and what not."

" So I did. Tch."

" God help 'em if I had to cook for 'em. Finish 'em
off altogether."

" Can anyone remember who it is that was to do the
cooking ? " the vicar's wife appealed.

" I can," replied Mr. Spriddle. " It was Mrs. Jones,
for 'oom I just now made an apology, due to 'er bein'
away."

" Oh dear. When will she be back ? "

" She did not confide," said Mr. Spriddle sadly.
" She merely said she was going away for an 'oliday,
and, should the call come, would I please explain and
apologise."

" I expect she'll be back soon," a lady suggested
helpfully. " After all, this is only a rehearsal. We're
not likely to have the real thing yet for quite a while."

" Ah! 'Oo knows ? 'Oo knows, ladies ? If you ask
me——"

The schoolmaster intervened.

" Will any lady volunteer to do the cooking, should
occasion arise before Mrs. Jones returns ? "

" I'll try," said a shy, fluffy-haired girl.

" Good. Thank you, Miss Harris."

The other duties were gone through until one came
that had been allocated to the last of the volunteers.
A babel of voices explained that the lady in question, a
Mrs. Higgins, had gone to live in another village.

Mr. Spriddle's voice rose above the uproar.

" Mrs. 'Iggings," he proclaimed, " 'as a loyle 'art. A

very loyle 'art Mrs. 'Iggings 'as. Twelve years she lived
'ere among us: and wot though she may 'ave moved
'ouse, depend upon it, she'll answer the call."

" Rubbish, man," exclaimed Mrs. Hunt. " How can
she answer the call when she won't hear it ? "

" Ow, well, o' course——"

" Come to that, how are *we* going to hear it ? It's all
right for those of us who are on the telephone. I'm not."

" I hexperienced no difficulty," said Mr. Spriddle, " in
transmittin' the call—except to you, Mrs. 'Unt. I
couldn't establish no direck contack, not with you."

" I told you, I was in my bath."

" Ar. I needs to be sure I can reach everyone quick,
'owever situated. 'Ow shall I be *sure* to rouse you,
Mrs. 'Unt ? "

" My bedroom window is over the front door. Stand
outside and let a bellow."

Mr. Spriddle stiffened. He disliked realism.

" I 'ope I shall succeed in my objeck without 'avin
recourse to no such measures."

At this point the Committee constituted itself a committee of ways and means—in other words, a free-for-all
—and after another ten minutes of it Honoria excused
herself on the grounds that she had to get ready my
supper: so I can record no more.

Still, I have not the least doubt that if—in the language
of Mr. Spriddle—the call comes, our village will give good
account of itself, and render yeoman service.

Cicely Hamilton

THE DETECTIVE IN FICTION

IT WAS TOWARDS the end of the Victorian era that English fiction gave birth to one of its most influential characters. Not only was his name destined to become a household word and his adventures read by millions, but he started a fashion in story-telling that endures to the present day. I am speaking, of course, of Sherlock Holmes.

With Sherlock Holmes began the era of the crime story —what may be called the reign of the detective in fiction. For reign it is: the detective, the tracker of criminals, has no rival in the affections of the reading public. Novels are written, now and then, round men of other trades and professions, but it is only the detective whose quota has no limit, only the detective who keeps relays of authors steadily at work and inspires a ceaseless flow of fiction.

I am not for a moment suggesting that when he wrote Sherlock Holmes, Conan Doyle did more than popularise detective fiction—this, of course, existed long before his day; Conan Doyle had many predecessors in the art and craft of the crime story. To name only a few of the most distinguished—there was Edgar Allan Poe, the American; Gaboriau, the Frenchman; Wilkie Collins, author of that classic crime story, *The Moonstone*. But there was something about the Baker Street detective—in part his personality, in part his methods—that caught the public fancy and created a demand for more fiction of the same type—more thrill combined with ingenuity. Thanks to that demand—that continuous demand—Sherlock Holmes has not wanted for disciples, some of them, by this time, almost as well known as himself. A varied collection of

disciples—professional and amateur, of all ranks and ages.
Englishmen and foreigners; members of the C.I.D. and
gentlemen at large; old men and young men, occasionally
a woman; doctors, ex-convicts, and at least one priest,
Father Brown.

It is, I think, likely that some among you—many
perhaps—will disagree with my estimate of Chesterton's
Father Brown series. I think I have read all of them,
most of them with interest; they are good stories, often
with a thrill to them, and written with the Chesterton
skill and mastery of English; but, considered as examples
of crime detection, I can't say I rank them very high.
In fact, my personal opinion is that several among them
are not detective stories at all in the accustomed sense
of the term. Father Brown, by virtue of his priestly
calling, and the insight it gives him into the passions and
temptations of his fellow-men, is able—as it were with a
flash—to pierce the veil of a mystery and perceive the
motive of a crime. He solves his problems through a
power not possessed by the ordinary man, and not by
the sifting of evidence or the tracing of clues. Father
Brown says so, and so it is; but the process whereby he
arrived at the truth is not always neatly comprehensible
by the ordinary mind—as it is in the case of a Sherlock
Holmes solution. It is, of course, quite legitimate to
write a crime story from that particular angle, but it will
not, I think, be a story of the real detective brand.

These remarks, I should add, do not apply to all the
solutions of Father Brown. There are exceptions, and
notably the excellent story of the postman murderer, who
was seen on his way to commit the crime but whom
nobody took any notice of—nobody remembered—just
because he was the postman who called at the house
every day. That, of course, is a real detective story, its
solution attainable by a process of ingenious reasoning.
It belongs to the same category as Edgar Allan Poe's little

masterpiece, *The Purloined Letter*, which also treats of the obvious that nobody notices. There, until the detective Dupin takes a hand, a stolen document remains undiscovered because no attempt has been made to hide it; it has merely been placed where anyone can see it, anyone can get at it—so nobody troubles to examine it.

Dupin, by the way, is the first of a long line of eccentric detectives; men with unusual personalities and sometimes with queer habits or tastes. Dupin's chief peculiarity was his strong dislike of daylight, his preference for living by artificial light and even for working in the dark; he put out his candle when he wanted to concentrate on a problem. Judging by the number of unusual personalities who have appeared, and still appear, in the pages of our crime literature, it is clear that the reading public likes a strain of the odd, the peculiar, in its man-hunters. To take a few examples; there is Edgar Wallace's Mr. Reeder, with his unfashionable whiskers, his umbrella, his mumbling speech, and his partiality for muffins; there is Albert Campion, Margery Allingham's amateur detective, who has a vacant face and talks like a cheerful idiot; there is Poirot, the conceited little Belgian, with his catchword about little grey cells. Anthony Weymouth's Inspector Treadgold is a sharp-nosed ferret of a man with a fondness for Latin quotation; and Lord Peter Wimsey, to say the least of it, is an unusual type of aristocrat. All of these are more or less eccentric personalities, and have, one and all, attained a wide popularity.

There is one remarkable single novel—which is also in its way a milestone—that is *Trent's Last Case* by E. C. Bentley, which by its skilful construction, its characterisation and original plot is surely worthy to be counted among the classics. The author, by the way, invented those nonsense rhymes with a curious metre which have been called after his second name of Clerihew.

The vogue for detective fiction is not confined, of course, to the English-speaking world; it is written in many different tongues. All the same, there is plenty of evidence to show that the English crime story stands highest in general esteem; again and again, when I have been travelling on the Continent, I have noticed translations of English detective novels displayed in shop windows, and displayed with a prominence that bore witness to their popularity.

Some years ago I was told that the translated works of Edgar Wallace had sold in Germany to the tune of a million and a half; that, of course, was before the enjoyment of books by foreign authors was discouraged by the Reich authorities. And a year or two ago, when I was travelling in northern Scandinavia, I alighted at a station in Swedish Lapland, well above the Arctic Circle; and lo and behold! on its modest bookstall I saw displayed some little paper-covered volumes bearing an English name; the name of an author who records the various exploits and adventures of a member of the C.I.D. Thanks to this international interest in our detective literature, there is, I should say, no British institution more familiar to the foreigner than Scotland Yard: its fame has spread round the world. And, with all due respect to Scotland Yard, its reputation abroad is due less to its merits—its undoubted merits—than to the skill of that numerous company of authors who use it as material for their tales of mystery and crime. The story-teller whose medium is English has, it would appear, a special ability for the writing of detective fiction. Call it a knack or call it a talent, it is something that makes his work acceptable, abroad as well as at home.

Miss Dorothy Sayers—than whom there can be no better authority on the subject—sees a connection between this English skill in the detective story and the traditional English respect for law and order. " The British legal code "—here I am quoting a passage by

Miss Sayers—" the British legal code with its tradition of ' sportsmanship ' and ' fair play for the criminal ' is particularly favourable to the production of detective fiction, allowing, as it does, sufficient rope to the criminal to provide a dingdong chase." And she goes on to point out that in certain other States of Europe, where the law is less respected than it is with us, the detective story is less frequent. There can be little doubt that Miss Sayers is right in connecting the law, and the popular view of it, with the output of crime stories; the detective would not be such a popular figure in the fiction of to-day if our criminal law were believed to be unjust and oppressive and if the guardians of the law were disliked by the average Englishman. When the law is held to be unjust and oppressive, then popular sympathy, as a matter of course, will be on the side of those who break and evade it—and popular fiction will follow suit. Then you get stories of what may be called the " Robin Hood " type —where the breaker of the law is a sympathetic character, only technically a criminal, who outwits the unpopular authorities. If authorship in the totalitarian states were allowed a free hand—if it could write what it liked without fear of the consequences—the probability is that it would produce a good deal of fiction on these lines, with sympathetic law-breakers escaping triumphant from the clutches of the secret police.

The crime-story has had a long innings. It is more than fifty years since the advent of Sherlock Holmes gave an impetus to detective literature; though it was not until after the last Great War that the output swelled to a veritable torrent and, incidentally, swamped the sentimental love story—which, until the detective arrived on the scene, was the subject-matter of most of our popular fiction. In time, no doubt, there will be a reaction and the fashion will change; the reading public will tire of perpetual clues and puzzles, as once it tired of a superfluity of love-interest; or the ranks of detective authors may be thinned by a growing difficulty in finding fresh plots and giving unexpected turns to mystery. But, if one may judge by publishers' advertisements and library shelves, that day of reaction is not yet; the public, at present, shows no symptom of boredom with its crimes and mysteries, the writers show no sign of exhaustion!